Betty Crocker's

RED SPOON COLLECTION™

BEST RECIPES FOR

GRILLING

PRENTICE HALL PRESS

New York   London   Toronto   Sydney   Tokyo

Published by Prentice Hall Press
A Division of Simon & Schuster, Inc.
Gulf+Western Building
One Gulf+Western Plaza
New York, NY 10023

Published simultaneously in Canada by
Prentice Hall Canada Inc.

PRENTICE HALL PRESS is a registered
trademark of Simon & Schuster, Inc.

BETTY CROCKER is a registered trademark of
General Mills, Inc.

RED SPOON COLLECTION is a trademark
of General Mills, Inc.

Library of Congress Cataloging-in-Publication

Betty Crocker's Red Spoon collection. Grilling.
p. cm.
Includes index.
ISBN 0-13-073024-6 : $9.95
1. Barbecue cookery.
TX840.B3B46 1989   88-26586
641.7′6—dc19   CIP

Manufactured in the United States of America

10 9 8 7 6 5 4 3 2 1

First Prentice Hall Press Edition

CONTENTS

INTRODUCTION   5

1 BEEF   9

2 PORK, LAMB AND VEAL   29

3 POULTRY   49

4 FISH AND SEAFOOD   64

5 VEGETABLES   80

6 BREADS AND DESSERTS   84

7 BARBECUE SAUCES   91

RED SPOON TIPS   97

INDEX   109

INTRODUCTION

Grilling

Food grilled outdoors has an incomparable flavor at any time of the year, and with this book in hand, grilling chops and steaks to perfection can be simple. But grilling doesn't stop with chops and steaks. With this book we bring you all-time favorites, such as Barbecued London Broil, Grilled Butterflied Shrimp, Wine-basted Hens and then go on to some scrumptious vegetables and mouthwatering, cheese-filled breads. The beauty of a grill is that it cooks more than the main course. For an event with show-stopping bravura, you can grill an entire meal from start to finish, *including* the dessert. On page 103 you will find suggested menus to suit every taste, budget and occasion.

If you are a newcomer to grilling, you should notice the wide range of grills available from which you can choose. Turn to pages 97–99 for a discussion of grills—the grills available for outdoor cooking, how different grills are designed, and how to cook on the grill of your choice; this will help you choose a grill to fit your needs. When you have installed your grill, you have all you need in the way of heavy equipment.

However, whether you are cooking on the smallest hibachi or the most elaborate electric grill, you will find certain utensils invaluable.

Essential Tools

The following are some essential tools for grilling:

- *Fire- and heat-resistant mitts* should be kept by the grill at all times. Wear them whenever you are tending to the coals or food on the grill. Remember that the fire can flare up at any time.
- *Tongs* are the best utensils to use when turning foods while they cook, because they hold the food rather than pierce it. Meat turned by a fork tends to lose some juiciness. In addition, use long-handled tongs so that you can tend food on the grill at a comfortable distance from the heat.
- *Basting brushes, spatulas and forks* are easiest to use at the grill side when they have long handles, too. Metal handles won't scorch.
- *A spray bottle of water* will help you keep the fire under control.

- *Meat thermometers* are a sure way to judge whether the food is cooked or whether it needs a few minutes longer. A kitchen-meat thermometer may be used but only for testing; do not use it as a gauge while cooking. A barbecue thermometer is designed to withstand the intense heat of the grill and can be left in the meat while it cooks.
- *Hinged wire baskets* (for grills) and *spit baskets* (for rotisseries) conveniently hold smaller pieces of food. A wire basket is especially handy for grilling fish, which easily falls apart with cooking.
- *Metal skewers* hold cubes or chunks of meat and/or vegetables together for kabobs. If your skewers have handles with wooden or painted decorations, keep the handles as far away from the heat as possible.
- *Small grill pans* can be set directly on the gridiron. Use them to hold basting sauces conveniently at hand, or as a warming dish for vegetables or breads.
- *Heavy-duty aluminum foil* can be shaped to serve as a makeshift casserole dish. Keep a good supply of foil on hand, as it can be used from cooking to cleanup.
- *Electric charcoal starters* get fires going quickly, without the hazards of liquid starter (see page 99).

Cooking on a Grill

Both gas and electric grills heat up quickly. If you are using a charcoal grill, remember that the fire won't be ready for anywhere from twenty-five to forty-five minutes after you light it, so plan your meal accordingly.

See page 99 for information on starting your electric, gas or charcoal grill, rotisserie or smoker.

When cooking over an open flame, roll up loose sleeves and tie back long hair. The firebox of your grill will get very hot, so keep flammable materials (including clothing) away from it. Set up your grill away from any walls and low ceilings, and always grill in a well-ventilated area. Finally, open hot covered dishes away from you to avoid a steam burn; foods cooked in tightly closed foil packets generate steam as they cook, too, so open them away from your face.

Cleanup

No one enjoys cleaning an outdoor grill, but you can make the job easier for yourself. If you clean the gridiron after each use, grease and charred food won't have a chance to build up. For a nonstick cooking surface, try brushing vegetable oil over the cooking grill and its underside. After cooking, a wire grill brush or scouring pad will scrub it clean. (Here is an old camper's trick: Aluminum foil, crumpled into a fist-size ball, can replace a scouring pad if one isn't handy.)

Some electric and gas grills are self-cleaning, so follow the manufacturer's cleaning instructions. Usually this will involve nothing more than closing the cover and heating the grill for fifteen minutes at maximum temperature. Burning grease and food particles off of the gridiron may not be as thorough as cleaning by hand, so you may want to give your self-cleaning grill a scrubbing from time to time.

No matter what sort of grill you have, you can line the firebox with heavy-duty aluminum foil. If you wish to raise the heat of the fire (or more properly, the coals), line the firebox with the shiny surface of the foil facing up; it will serve as a heat reflector. The foil will keep drippings from cooking onto the firebox surface and, if you are using charcoal, will hold the ashes in a package that's a snap to throw away.

Look through the Red Spoon Tips section (page 97). There you'll find explanations of cuts of meat, safety tips, entertaining advice, tests for doneness, and a world of fresh ideas you will refer to time after time. There are many ways to be imaginative when grilling, more than you might realize, and we hope you enjoy exploring them with us.

THE BETTY CROCKER EDITORS

BEEF

Hamburgers

1 pound ground beef
3 tablespoons water or milk
2 to 3 tablespoons finely chopped onion
½ teaspoon salt
¼ teaspoon pepper

Mix all ingredients. Shape mixture into 4 patties, each about 4 inches in diameter.

Grill patties about 4 inches from medium coals, turning once, until desired doneness, 5 to 7 minutes on each side for medium. Serve in split hamburger buns, if desired.

Hamburgers Supreme

2 tablespoons instant minced onion
2 tablespoons water
1 pound ground beef
1 egg
¼ cup catsup
⅓ cup fine dry bread crumbs
*2 tablespoons finely chopped mustard
   pickle*
1 tablespoon Worcestershire sauce
1 teaspoon salt
¼ teaspoon pepper

Mix all ingredients. Shape mixture into 6 patties; chill thoroughly. Grill 4 inches from hot coals 6 minutes on each side. Serve in toasted hamburger buns, if desired.

Note: To toast hamburger buns, spread buns with margarine or butter and grill, cut sides down, until golden brown, about 4 minutes.

Following pages: Hamburgers Supreme

Fiesta Burgers

Fiesta Filling (below)
Avocado Topping (below)
1 1/2 pounds ground beef
1/4 cup dry bread crumbs
2 tablespoons water
1 tablespoon Worcestershire sauce
1/2 teaspoon salt
1/4 teaspoon pepper
1 egg

Prepare Fiesta Filling and Avocado Topping. Mix remaining ingredients. Shape mixture into 12 patties, each about 4 inches in diameter. Spread each of 6 patties with about 2 tablespoons filling to within 1/2 inch of edge; top with a remaining patty and seal edge firmly.

Grill patties about 4 inches from medium coals, turning once, until desired doneness, 5 to 7 minutes on each side for medium. Serve with Avocado Topping. Serve in hamburger buns, if desired.

FIESTA FILLING

1/4 cup finely chopped onions
1/4 cup finely chopped tomato
1/4 cup finely chopped green chilies

Mix all ingredients.

AVOCADO TOPPING

1 small avocado, cut up
1/4 cup dairy sour cream
1 tablespoon lemon juice
1/8 to 1/4 teaspoon red pepper sauce

Beat all ingredients with hand beater until smooth.

Filled Hamburgers

1 1/2 pounds ground beef
1/4 cup dry bread crumbs
2 tablespoons water
1 tablespoon Worcestershire sauce
1/2 teaspoon salt
1/4 teaspoon pepper
1 egg
Fillings*

Mix all ingredients except Fillings. Shape mixture into 12 patties, each about 4 inches in diameter. Top each of 6 patties with one of the Fillings, spreading to within 1/2 inch of edge; top with a remaining patty and seal edge firmly.

Grill patties about 4 inches from medium coals, turning once, until desired doneness, 5 to 7 minutes on each side for medium. Serve in split hamburger buns, if desired.

*Fillings: 1 tablespoon finely chopped onion, 1 tablespoon chopped tomato, 1 tablespoon shredded Cheddar cheese or 1 to 2 teaspoons prepared horseradish.

Cheeseburgers Deluxe

Mushroom Topping (below)
1 1/2 pounds ground beef
1/2 cup shredded Cheddar cheese (about 2 ounces)
1/1 cup dry bread crumbs
1/4 cup water
1 teaspoon lemon pepper

Prepare Mushroom Topping; keep warm or reheat after grilling Cheeseburgers. Mix remaining ingredients. Shape mixture into 8 patties, each about 4 inches in diameter.

Grill patties about 4 inches from medium coals, turning once, until desired doneness, 4 to 6 minutes on each side for medium. Serve each with Mushroom Topping. Serve in hamburger buns, if desired.

MUSHROOM TOPPING

8 ounces small mushrooms, cut into halves
1/4 cup chopped green onions (with tops)
1 tablespoon snipped parsley
2 tablespoons margarine or butter
Grated Parmesan cheese

Cook and stir all ingredients except cheese in 10-inch skillet until mushrooms are tender, 2 to 3 minutes; sprinkle with cheese.

Lemon Burgers

1 teaspoon instant beef bouillon
¼ cup hot water
1 pound ground beef
¼ cup dry bread crumbs
1 teaspoon grated lemon peel
¼ teaspoon ground nutmeg
¼ teaspoon salt
¼ teaspoon pepper
1 egg

Dissolve instant bouillon in hot water. Mix bouillon and remaining ingredients. Shape mixture into 4 patties, each about 4 inches in diameter.

Grill patties about 4 inches from medium coals, turning once, until desired doneness, 5 to 7 minutes on each side for medium. Serve in toasted split hamburger buns (page 9) and garnish with lemon slices, if desired.

Tortilla Burgers

1 pound ground beef
½ cup refried beans
¼ cup chopped green chilies
¼ cup chopped onions
1 tablespoon snipped parsley
6 seven-inch flour tortillas
Taco sauce

Mix all ingredients except tortillas and taco sauce. Shape mixture into 6 oval patties, each about 4 inches long and 3 inches wide.

Grill patties about 4 inches from medium coals, turning once, until desired doneness, 5 to 7 minutes on each side for medium. Wrap tortillas in aluminum foil. Heat on grill until warm, 4 to 6 minutes. Serve patties in tortillas with taco sauce. Garnish with chopped tomato, more snipped parsley and dairy sour cream, if desired.

Colossal Burgers

1 1/2 pounds ground beef
3 tablespoons water
1 teaspoon salt
1/2 teaspoon ground sage
1/4 cup chopped green onions (with tops)
1 tablespoon prepared horseradish
1 tablespoon prepared mustard
1 package (3 ounces) cream cheese,
  softened

Mix ground beef, water, salt and sage. Divide mixture into halves. Shape each half into patty, about 8 inches in diameter, on waxed paper. Mix remaining ingredients. Spread mixture over 1 patty to within 1/2 inch of edge. Invert remaining patty on mixture; remove top sheet of waxed paper. Seal edge firmly. Invert patty on well-greased hinged wire grill basket; remove waxed paper.

Grill patty about 4 inches from medium coals, turning 2 or 3 times, until desired doneness, 10 to 12 minutes on each side for medium. Cut into wedges. Garnish with green onions and cherry tomatoes, if desired.

Curried Beef and Vegetable Kabobs

3/4 cup plain yogurt
1/4 cup lemon juice
1/4 cup finely chopped onion
1 to 2 teaspoons curry powder
1 teaspoon ground cumin
1 teaspoon salt
1/4 teaspoon pepper
1 clove garlic, crushed
1 1/2-pound beef boneless bottom or top
  round steak, cut into 1-inch cubes
1 green pepper, cut into 1-inch pieces
12 whole mushrooms
12 cherry tomatoes

Mix yogurt, lemon juice, onion, curry, cumin, salt, pepper and garlic; pour over beef cubes. Cover and refrigerate, turning beef 2 or 3 times, at least 4 hours.

Remove beef; reserve marinade. Thread beef cubes about 1/4 inch apart on each of 3 metal skewers. Alternate pepper pieces, mushrooms and tomatoes on each of 3 metal skewers, leaving space between foods.

Cover and grill beef kabobs 4 to 5 inches from medium coals, turning and brushing 2 or 3 times with reserved marinade, until desired doneness, 15 to 20 minutes for medium. Cover and grill vegetable kabobs, turning and brushing 2 or 3 times with reserved marinade, until vegetables are crisp-tender, 10 to 20 minutes.

Following pages: Curried Beef and Vegetable Kabobs

Beef on Skewers

1 cup tomato juice
¼ cup vinegar
2 tablespoons prepared mustard
1 teaspoon sugar
1 teaspoon salt
¼ teaspoon pepper
1½-pound beef boneless sirloin steak, cut
*   into 1-inch cubes*
½ pound mushroom caps
1 large green pepper, cut into 1-inch
*   pieces*
1 pint cherry tomatoes
½ fresh pineapple, cut into pieces

Mix tomato juice, vinegar and seasonings; pour over beef cubes. Cover and refrigerate at least 2 hours.

Remove beef; reserve marinade. Alternate beef cubes, vegetables and pineapple on each of 6 to 8 metal skewers, leaving space between foods.

Cover and grill kabobs 4 to 5 inches from medium coals, turning 2 or 3 times and brushing 4 or 5 times with reserved marinade, until beef is of desired doneness, 20 to 30 minutes for medium.

Beer-barbecued Steak

1 bottle (7 ounces) beer
¼ cup chili sauce
2 tablespoons vegetable oil
1 tablespoon soy sauce
2 teaspoons Dijon-style mustard
¼ teaspoon red pepper sauce
⅛ teaspoon liquid smoke
1 small onion, coarsely chopped
1 clove garlic, crushed
3-pound beef sirloin steak, 1 to 1½
*   inches thick*

Mix all ingredients except beef steak. Heat to boiling; reduce heat. Simmer uncovered 30 minutes.

Brush beef with beer mixture. Cover and grill beef 4 to 5 inches from medium coals, turning 2 or 3 times and brushing 4 or 5 times with beer mixture, until desired doneness, 25 to 30 minutes for medium. Cut into serving pieces. Serve with remaining beer mixture as sauce.

Charcoal-broiled Steak

For each serving:

¾-, 1- or 1½-inch-thick beef steaks*

Slash diagonally outer edge of fat on beef steak at 1-inch intervals to prevent curling (do not cut into lean). Grill beef 4 to 5 inches from medium coals, turning once or twice, until medium; cook ¾-inch-thick steak 10 to 20 minutes, 1-inch-thick steak 18 to 25 minutes and 1½-inch-thick steak 25 to 35 minutes.

*Allow ⅓ pound per serving with bone, ¼ pound per serving for boneless cuts.

Steak au Poivre

6 TO 8 SERVINGS

1 to 2 tablespoons peppercorns, crushed
2½-pound beef sirloin steak, 1 to 1½
  inches thick
¾ cup water
¼ cup chopped green onions (with tops)
2 tablespoons margarine or butter
1 tablespoon catsup
1 tablespoon steak sauce
1 teaspoon instant beef bouillon
2 tablespoons brandy

Press peppercorns in both sides of beef steak. Grill beef 4 to 5 inches from medium coals, turning 2 or 3 times, until desired doneness, 30 to 35 minutes for medium. Heat remaining ingredients except brandy to boiling, stirring constantly; remove from heat. Stir in brandy. Cut beef into serving pieces. Garnish with red and green cherry peppers and celery leaves, if desired. Serve with brandy mixture.

MICROWAVE REHEAT DIRECTIONS: For 1 serving, place refrigerated beef and sauce on microwaveproof plate. Cover loosely and microwave on medium (50%) until hot, 1½ to 2½ minutes. Let stand 1 minute. For 2 servings, microwave 3 to 4 minutes.

Following pages: Steak au Poivre

Barbecued London Broil

1/3 cup white vinegar
1/3 cup vegetable oil
3 tablespoons packed brown sugar
3 tablespoons soy sauce
2 medium onions, sliced
1 clove garlic, crushed
1/2 teaspoon coarsely ground pepper
1 1/2-pound beef flank steak

Mix all ingredients except beef flank steak; pour over beef. Cover and refrigerate, turning beef 2 or 3 times, at least 4 hours.

Remove beef and onions; reserve marinade. Cover and grill beef 4 to 5 inches from medium coals, turning and brushing 2 or 3 times with reserved marinade, until desired doneness, 10 to 15 minutes for medium. Cook and stir onions in grill pan on grill until warm. Cut beef diagonally across the grain into very thin slices; top with onions.

Ranch Steak

1/2 cup finely chopped onion
1/2 cup dry red wine
2 tablespoons vegetable oil
1 teaspoon dry mustard
1 teaspoon salt
1/4 teaspoon red pepper sauce
1 clove garlic, crushed
1 1/2-pound beef boneless bottom or top round steak, about 1 inch thick
1/2 cup chili sauce

Mix all ingredients except beef steak and chili sauce; pour over beef. Cover and refrigerate, turning beef 2 or 3 times, at least 4 hours.

Remove beef; stir chili sauce into marinade. Cover and grill beef 4 to 5 inches from medium coals, turning and brushing 2 or 3 times with marinade mixture, until desired doneness, 20 to 30 minutes for medium. Cut beef into 1/2-inch-thick slices. Heat remaining marinade mixture in grill pan on grill. Serve with beef.

MICROWAVE REHEAT DIRECTIONS: For 1 serving, place refrigerated beef and sauce on microwaveproof plate. Cover loosely and microwave on medium (50%) until hot, 1 1/2 to 2 1/2 minutes. Let stand 1 minute. For 2 servings, microwave 3 to 4 minutes.

Liver Venetian

½ cup dry red wine
¼ cup chopped green onions (with tops)
2 tablespoons vegetable oil
1 tablespoon lemon juice
½ teaspoon dried sage leaves, crushed
½ teaspoon dried basil leaves
¼ teaspoon pepper
1½-pound beef liver, about 1½ inches thick

Mix all ingredients except beef liver; pour over liver. Cover and refrigerate, turning liver once, at least 1 hour.

Remove liver; reserve marinade. Cover and grill liver 4 to 5 inches from medium coals, turning and brushing 2 or 3 times with reserved marinade, until desired doneness, 15 to 20 minutes for medium (160°). Spoon remaining chopped green onions from marinade over liver. Cut liver into thin slices.

Tomato-glazed Short Ribs

4 pounds beef short ribs, cut into serving pieces
Unseasoned meat tenderizer
1 can (8 ounces) tomato sauce
¼ cup red wine
1 teaspoon onion powder
⅛ teaspoon red pepper sauce
2 cloves garlic, crushed

Sprinkle beef ribs with meat tenderizer as directed on label. Mix remaining ingredients; pour over beef. Cover and refrigerate, turning beef 2 or 3 times, at least 4 hours.

Remove beef; reserve marinade. Cover and grill beef 4 to 5 inches from medium coals, turning and brushing 4 or 5 times with reserved marinade, until desired doneness, 35 to 45 minutes for medium.

MICROWAVE REHEAT DIRECTIONS: For 1 serving, place refrigerated beef on microwaveproof plate. Cover loosely and microwave on high (100%) until hot, 2 to 3 minutes. Let stand 1 minute. For 2 servings, microwave 3 to 5 minutes.

Following pages: Tomato-glazed Short Ribs

Beef Tenderloin Roast

13 OR 14 SERVINGS

4-pound beef tenderloin
Melted margarine or butter

Cover and grill tenderloin 4 to 5 inches from medium coals, turning and brushing 2 or 3 times with margarine, until desired doneness, 20 to 25 minutes for rare, 30 to 35 minutes for medium rare, 35 to 40 minutes for medium. Cut into serving pieces.

Marinated Rump Roast

12 TO 16 SERVINGS

1 cup orange juice
1 cup tomato juice
1/4 cup vegetable oil
1 clove garlic, crushed
2 teaspoons salt
1/2 teaspoon ground allspice
1/4 teaspoon chili powder
3- to 4-pound beef rolled rump roast
3 tablespoons flour
1/3 cup water

Mix juices, oil, garlic, salt, allspice and chili powder; pour over beef roast. Cover and refrigerate, turning beef 2 or 3 times, at least 4 hours.

Remove beef; reserve 2 cups marinade. Insert spit rod lengthwise through center of beef; hold firmly in place with adjustable holding forks. Cook beef on rotisserie about 4 inches from low heat until desired doneness, 1 to 1 1/2 hours for medium (160°).

Mix flour and water; stir into reserved marinade. Heat to boiling, stirring constantly. Boil and stir 1 minute. Cut beef into thin slices; serve marinade mixture over beef.

Rotisserie Beef Roast

5-pound beef boneless rolled rib roast*
Peppy Tomato Barbecue Sauce or Wine
  Barbecue Sauce (below)

Insert spit rod lengthwise through center of rolled rib roast; hold firmly in place with adjustable holding forks. Place foil drip pan under roasting area.

Cover and cook beef on rotisserie about 4 inches from low heat; cook 1¾ to 2 hours for rare (140°), 2½ to 3 hours for medium (160°) and 3¼ hours for well done (170°). Brush beef 2 or 3 times with Peppy Tomato Barbecue Sauce during last 15 minutes of cooking. Remove beef from rotisserie when meat thermometer registers 5° to 10° lower than desired doneness. Remove spit rod; let beef stand in warm place 15 minutes before carving. Garnish with tomato rose and curly endive and serve with any remaining sauce, if desired.

*For roasts weighing less or more, consult the Timetable on page 109.

PEPPY TOMATO BARBECUE SAUCE

½ cup chili sauce
1 tablespoon vinegar
1 tablespoon molasses
1 teaspoon garlic salt
¼ teaspoon red pepper sauce

Mix all ingredients.

WINE BARBECUE SAUCE

⅓ cup dry red wine
⅓ cup chili sauce
1 tablespoon vegetable oil
1 clove garlic, crushed
¼ teaspoon red pepper sauce

Mix all ingredients.

Pepper and Onion Roast

3-pound beef cross rib pot roast, about
  1 1/2 inches thick
1 envelope (.8 ounce) meat marinade
2 large red or green peppers, cut into
  1/4-inch strips
1 large white or red onion, cut into
  halves and thinly sliced
1/4 cup olive or vegetable oil
1 clove garlic, crushed
1 tablespoon vinegar
1 teaspoon dried oregano leaves
1/2 teaspoon salt
1/4 teaspoon pepper

Marinate beef roast as directed on marinade envelope. Cook and stir red peppers and onion in oil in 10-inch skillet over medium heat until crisp-tender, 3 to 5 minutes. Stir in remaining ingredients; remove from heat.

Cover and grill beef 4 to 5 inches from medium coals, turning 2 or 3 times, until desired doneness, 40 to 50 minutes for medium. Heat and stir pepper and onion mixture on grill until warm. Top beef with pepper and onion mixture; cut beef into thin slices.

· 2 ·

PORK, LAMB AND VEAL

Glazed Franks

For each serving:

1 frankfurter
1 tablespoon packed brown sugar
1½ teaspoons horseradish

Make diagonal cuts in frankfurter almost through to bottom. Mix brown sugar and horseradish; brush on frankfurter. Grill 5 to 6 inches from medium coals, turning 4 or 5 times, until heated through, 12 to 15 minutes.

STUFFED FRANKFURTERS: Omit brown sugar and horseradish. For each serving, cook 1 slice bacon 2 minutes each side. Cut frankfurter lengthwise almost through to bottom. Fill each frankfurter with one of the following: 1 green onion, 1 cantaloupe spear, 3 mandarin orange segments, 1 pineapple spear, thin slice dill pickle, crunchy peanut butter or creamy peanut butter and salted peanuts, shredded Cheddar cheese, 3 apple slices and 1 slice process American cheese.

Grilled Pork Chops

For each serving:

1- to 1½-inch-thick pork chop
Sauce (pages 92 and 93), if desired
Salt and pepper, if desired

Trim excess fat from pork chop. Grill pork 4 inches from medium coals until done and no longer pink in center (170°), 60 to 70 minutes; turn pork 4 or 5 times. Brush with a sauce, if desired, after 30 minutes of grilling. Season with salt and pepper, if desired, after removing from grill.

Marinated Pork Chops

4 SERVINGS

3 tablespoons packed brown sugar
3 tablespoons bourbon
3 tablespoons soy sauce
¼ teaspoon ground ginger
4 pork loin or rib chops, ¾ inch thick

Mix all ingredients except pork chops; pour over pork. Cover and refrigerate, turning pork 2 or 3 times, at least 4 hours.

Remove pork; reserve marinade. Cover and grill pork 5 to 6 inches from medium coals, turning 3 or 4 times and brushing 2 or 3 times with reserved marinade, until pork is done and no longer pink in center (170°), 20 to 30 minutes. Serve with hot buttered noodles sprinkled with grated Parmesan cheese, if desired.

Peanut-stuffed Pork Chops

8 SERVINGS

8 pork rib chops, about 1 inch thick
1 cup croutons
1/2 cup finely chopped salted peanuts
2 tablespoons instant minced onion
2 tablespoons finely snipped parsley
1/2 to 1 teaspoon crushed red chili
  pepper
1/3 cup margarine or butter, melted
1 tablespoon water
3/4 teaspoon salt
1/2 cup apple jelly
1 tablespoon lemon juice

Cut pocket in each pork chop on bone side.

Mix croutons, peanuts, onion, parsley and chili pepper in bowl. Mix margarine, water and salt. Pour over crouton mixture; toss. Stuff pork chop pockets with crouton mixture. Heat jelly and lemon juice just to boiling, stirring constantly.

Cover and grill pork 5 to 6 inches from medium coals until done and no longer pink in center (170°), 50 to 60 minutes; turn pork 3 or 4 times and brush with jelly mixture 2 or 3 times during last 30 minutes of grilling.

Smoked Pork Chops

5 SERVINGS

1 cup apple cider
1/4 cup chopped green onions (with tops)
2 tablespoons lemon juice
5 small smoked pork loin or rib chops,
  1/2 inch thick
2 teaspoons cornstarch
1 can (20 ounces) sliced apples, drained

Mix apple cider, green onions and lemon juice; pour over pork chops. Cover and refrigerate, turning pork 2 or 3 times, at least 1 hour.

Remove pork; reserve marinade. Cover and grill pork 5 to 6 inches from medium coals, turning 3 or 4 times, until pork is done and no longer pink in center (170°), 15 to 20 minutes. Stir 1/4 cup reserved marinade into cornstarch; mix in remaining marinade. Cook over medium heat, stirring constantly, until mixture thickens and boils. Boil and stir 1 minute. Stir in apple slices; heat through. Serve with pork.

Following pages: Grilled Pork Chop

Texas Pork Steaks

1 teaspoon chili powder
1/2 teaspoon garlic powder
1/2 teaspoon dry mustard
1/2 teaspoon salt
1/4 teaspoon pepper
2 pounds pork blade or arm steaks, 1/2
  inch thick

Mix all ingredients except pork steaks; rub on pork. Cover and grill pork 5 to 6 inches from medium coals, turning 3 or 4 times, until pork is done and no longer pink in center (170°), 25 to 35 minutes.

MICROWAVE REHEAT DIRECTIONS: For 1 serving, place refrigerated pork on microwaveproof plate. Cover loosely and microwave on medium (50%) until hot, 1 1/2 to 2 1/2 minutes. Let stand 1 minute. For 2 servings, microwave 3 to 4 minutes.

Italian Sausage Kabobs

6 SERVINGS

1/2 cup pizza sauce
1 tablespoon dried basil leaves
1 tablespoon vegetable oil
1 1/2 pounds Italian-style sausages, cut
  into 1 1/2-inch pieces
2 medium zucchini, cut into 1-inch pieces
1 medium red pepper, cut into 1 1/2-inch
  pieces
1 medium green pepper, cut into
  1 1/2-inch pieces
6 large pimiento-stuffed olives

Mix pizza sauce, basil and oil; reserve. Cook sausage pieces in 10-inch skillet over medium heat until partially cooked, about 10 minutes; drain. Alternate sausage pieces, zucchini pieces, and red and green pepper pieces on each of 6 metal skewers, leaving space between foods. Place olive on tip of each skewer.

Cover and grill kabobs 5 to 6 inches from medium coals, turning and brushing 2 or 3 times with reserved pizza sauce mixture, until sausage is done and vegetables are crisp-tender, 20 to 25 minutes.

Smoked Ham with Maple Glaze

¼ cup maple syrup
1 teaspoon dry mustard
½ teaspoon ground allspice
1 fully cooked smoked ham slice, 1 inch thick (about 2 pounds)
Whole cloves

Mix maple syrup, mustard and allspice; reserve. Slash ham at 1-inch intervals; insert cloves. Cover and grill ham 5 to 6 inches from medium coals, turning and brushing 2 or 3 times with syrup mixture, until ham is done (140°), 20 to 25 minutes. Remove cloves from ham; brush ham with syrup mixture. Cut into serving pieces. Garnish with spiced peaches and celery leaves, if desired.

Smokehouse Spareribs

3 cups hickory wood chips
½ cup vinegar
½ cup Worcestershire sauce
½ cup margarine or butter, melted
½ teaspoon salt
¼ teaspoon red pepper sauce
2 racks fresh pork spareribs (about 6 pounds)

Cover hickory chips with water. Let stand 30 minutes; drain. Mix remaining ingredients except pork spareribs in separate bowl; brush on spareribs. Arrange hot coals around edge of firebox; place foil drip pan under grilling area. Add half of the hickory chips to hot coals.

Cover and grill spareribs, bone sides down, over drip pan and 5 to 6 inches from medium coals until done and meat begins to pull away from bone (170°), 1¾ to 2¼ hours; turn and brush spareribs every 10 minutes with vinegar mixture during last 40 minutes of grilling. Add soaked hickory chips and coals every 30 minutes to maintain smoke and even heat. Cut spareribs into serving pieces.

Barbecued Ribs

4 1/2-pound rack fresh pork loin back ribs
3 cups water
1/2 cup soy sauce
1 tablespoon plus 1 1/2 teaspoons
   cornstarch
Sweet-and-Sour Sauce (below)

Place pork back ribs in Dutch oven; add water. Heat to boiling; reduce heat. Cover and simmer 5 minutes. Remove ribs; drain. Mix soy sauce and cornstarch; brush on ribs. Continue brushing both sides of ribs with soy sauce mixture every 10 minutes, allowing mixture to penetrate pork, until mixture is gone.

Cover and grill ribs 5 to 6 inches from medium coals, brushing with Sweet and Sour Sauce every 3 minutes, until ribs are done and meat begins to pull away from bone (170°), 15 to 20 minutes. Cut into serving pieces. Serve with remaining sauce.

SWEET-AND-SOUR SAUCE

1 cup water
1 cup catsup
1/4 cup packed brown sugar
1/4 cup vinegar
1/4 cup Worcestershire sauce
1 tablespoon celery seed
1 teaspoon chili powder
1 teaspoon salt
Few drops red pepper sauce
Dash of pepper

Heat all ingredients to boiling; remove from heat.

Smoked Chutney Spareribs

3 cups hickory wood chips
1 cup chutney
2 tablespoons lemon juice
2 tablespoons Worcestershire sauce
½ teaspoon salt
¼ teaspoon red pepper sauce
3-pound rack fresh pork spareribs, cut
  into halves

Cover hickory chips with water. Let stand 30 minutes; drain. Mix remaining ingredients except pork spareribs in separate bowl; pour over spareribs. Cover and refrigerate, turning spareribs once, at least 1 hour.

Remove spareribs; reserve marinade. Add 1 cup hickory chips to hot charcoal. Fill smoker water pan with water. Place spareribs, bone sides down, on rack about 6 inches from water pan over coals.

Cover smoker and smoke-cook spareribs, brushing with reserved marinade every hour, until spareribs are done and meat begins to pull away from bones (170°), 3 to 4 hours. Add charcoal and soaked hickory chips every hour (add water to pan during cooking if necessary). Cut spareribs into serving pieces. Serve with any remaining marinade, if desired.

Spit-barbecued Ribs

1 cup soy sauce
½ cup dry white wine or pineapple juice
2 tablespoons honey
1 clove garlic, crushed
3- to 4-pound rack fresh pork loin back
  ribs
¼ cup honey

Mix all ingredients except pork back ribs and ¼ cup honey; pour over ribs. Cover and refrigerate, turning ribs 2 or 3 times, at least 4 hours.

Remove ribs. Thread ribs on spit rod; hold firmly in place with adjustable holding forks. Cover and cook ribs on rotisserie about 4 inches from low heat until done and meat begins to pull away from bone (170°), 1¼ to 1¾ hours; brush ribs 2 or 3 times with ¼ cup honey during last 15 minutes of cooking. Cut into serving pieces.

Following pages: Barbecued Ribs

Roast Pork and Orange Sauce

1 can (12 ounces) frozen orange juice
  concentrate, thawed
2 cups water
1/2 cup packed brown sugar
2 teaspoons salt
1 teaspoon crushed dried marjoram
  leaves
1 teaspoon crushed dried rosemary leaves
1/2 teaspoon coarsely ground pepper
6-pound fresh pork sirloin roast, hipbone
  removed and backbone loosened
1/4 cup water
1 tablespoon cornstarch

Mix all ingredients except pork roast, 1/4 cup water and the cornstarch; pour over pork. Cover and refrigerate, turning pork occasionally, at least 8 hours.

Remove pork; reserve marinade. Tie pork with heavy string. Insert spit rod lengthwise through center of pork; hold firmly in place with adjustable holding forks. Cover and cook pork on rotisserie about 4 inches from low heat until done and no longer pink in center (170°), 2 1/2 to 3 hours; brush pork 2 or 3 times with reserved marinade during last 30 minutes of cooking.

Stir 1/4 cup water into cornstarch; stir in remaining marinade. Cook over medium heat, stirring constantly, until mixture thickens and boils. Boil and stir 1 minute. Cut pork into serving pieces; serve marinade mixture with pork. Garnish with orange slices, spiced crabapple and parsley, if desired.

Rotisserie Polynesian Pork

12 SERVINGS

1/2 cup pineapple juice
1/2 cup vegetable oil
1/2 cup dark corn syrup
1/4 cup lime juice
1 small clove garlic, finely chopped
2 tablespoons packed brown sugar
1 tablespoon prepared mustard
1 tablespoon soy sauce
2 teaspoons salt
1 teaspoon ground coriander
1/2 teaspoon ground ginger
4-pound fresh pork boneless blade Boston
   roast, rolled and tied

Mix all ingredients except pork roast; pour over pork. Cover and refrigerate, turning pork occasionally, at least 8 hours.

Remove pork. Insert spit rod lengthwise through center of pork; hold firmly in place with adjustable holding forks. Cover and cook pork on rotisserie about 4 inches from low heat until done and no longer pink in center (170°), 3 to 3 1/2 hours. Cut into serving pieces.

Peachy Ham on the Rotisserie

6 SERVINGS

1/2 cup peach preserves
1 tablespoon chili sauce
1 tablespoon lemon juice
1/8 teaspoon ground cloves
1/8 teaspoon liquid smoke
1 1/2-pound fully cooked boneless smoked
   ham

Mix all ingredients except ham; reserve. Insert spit rod lengthwise through center of ham; hold firmly in place with adjustable holding forks.

Cover and cook ham on rotisserie about 4 inches from low heat until done (140°), 50 to 60 minutes; brush ham 2 or 3 times with reserved peach preserve mixture during last 15 minutes of cooking. Cut into serving pieces. Serve any remaining peach preserve mixture with ham. Garnish with peach halves sprinkled with snipped parsley, if desired.

Following pages: Roast Pork and Orange Sauce

Lamb and Vegetable Kabobs

1/2 cup vegetable oil
1/3 cup lemon juice
1 clove garlic, finely chopped
2 teaspoons salt
1 teaspoon dried dill weed
1/4 teaspoon coarsely ground pepper
1 1/2 pounds lamb boneless shoulder, cut
    into 1 1/4-inch cubes
4 small whole tomatoes
2 large ears corn, cut into 2-inch pieces

Mix oil, lemon juice, garlic, salt, dill weed and pepper; pour over lamb cubes. Cover and refrigerate, turning lamb 2 or 3 times, at least 4 hours.

Remove lamb; reserve marinade. Thread lamb cubes and vegetables separately on metal skewers, leaving space between foods. Insert 2 skewers parallel and about 1/2 inch apart through center of tomatoes to keep them from slipping when they are turned.

Cover and grill lamb kabobs 5 to 6 inches from medium coals, turning once, until done, about 20 minutes. Cover and grill vegetable kabobs, brushing 2 or 3 times with reserved marinade, 15 minutes.

Leg of Lamb Barbecue

4- to 5-pound leg of lamb, boned
2 small cloves garlic, peeled and slivered
1/2 cup red wine vinegar
1/3 cup vegetable oil
1/3 cup packed brown sugar
2 tablespoons dried tarragon leaves
1 teaspoon salt
2 green onions (with tops), cut into
    2-inch slices
1 can (8 ounces) tomato sauce

Trim excess fat from lamb; if necessary, cut lamb to lie flat. Cut 4 or 5 slits in lamb with tip of sharp knife; insert garlic slivers in slits. Mix remaining ingredients except tomato sauce; pour over lamb. Cover and refrigerate, turning lamb 2 or 3 times, at least 8 hours.

Remove lamb; stir tomato sauce into marinade. Cover and grill lamb 5 to 6 inches from medium coals until done (175°), 50 to 60 minutes; turn lamb every 10 minutes and brush 2 or 3 times with marinade mixture during last 10 minutes of grilling. Remove garlic slivers; cut lamb into serving pieces. Garnish with tomato wedges and parsley, if desired.

Grilled Lamb Chops

2 pounds lamb shoulder chops, about 1/2
  inch thick
Orange-Ginger Sauce, Mint Garlic Sauce
  or Red Currant Sauce (below)

Cover and grill lamb chops 5 to 6 inches from medium coals, turning and brushing 2 or 3 times with sauce until lamb is of desired doneness, 12 to 18 minutes for medium. Serve with any remaining sauce.

ORANGE-GINGER SAUCE

1/4 cup frozen orange juice concentrate,
  thawed
1/4 cup soy sauce
1 teaspoon crushed fresh gingerroot

Mix all ingredients.

MINT-GARLIC SAUCE

1/2 cup mint-flavored apple jelly
2 tablespoons water
2 cloves garlic, crushed

Heat all ingredients over medium heat, stirring constantly, until jelly is melted.

RED CURRANT SAUCE

1/2 cup red currant jelly
1 tablespoon prepared mustard
1 tablespoon soy sauce

Heat all ingredients over medium heat, stirring constantly, until jelly is melted.

Following pages: Leg of Lamb Barbecue and Parmesan Slices

Veal and Apples on Skewers

8 SERVINGS

*1 can (6 ounces) frozen orange juice
    concentrate, thawed*
½ cup honey
¼ cup chopped crystallized ginger
¾ teaspoon dried marjoram leaves
*2 pounds veal boneless shoulder, cut into
    1-inch cubes*
4 medium apples, each cut into fourths

Mix orange juice concentrate, honey, ginger and marjoram; pour over veal cubes. Cover and refrigerate, turning veal occasionally, at least 2 hours.

Remove veal; reserve marinade. Alternate veal cubes and apples on each of 8 metal skewers, leaving space between foods. Cover and grill kabobs 5 to 6 inches from medium coals, turning and brushing 4 or 5 times with reserved marinade, until veal is brown and apples are tender, about 30 minutes.

· 3 ·

POULTRY

Simple Grilled Chicken

6 SERVINGS

1 teaspoon salt
1/4 teaspoon pepper
3-pound broiler-fryer chicken, cut up
1/4 cup margarine or butter, melted

Mix salt and pepper; rub on chicken pieces. Cover and grill chicken, bone sides down, 5 to 6 inches from medium coals, 15 to 30 minutes; turn chicken. Cover and grill, turning and brushing 2 or 3 times with margarine, until chicken is done, 20 to 40 minutes longer.

Lemon Chicken

6 SERVINGS

1/2 cup dry white wine
1/4 cup lemon juice
2 tablespoons vegetable oil
1 teaspoon paprika
1 lemon, thinly sliced
1 clove garlic, crushed
3-pound broiler-fryer chicken, cut up
1 lemon, thinly sliced
Paprika

Mix wine, lemon juice, oil, 1 teaspoon paprika, 1 lemon and the garlic; pour over chicken pieces. Cover and refrigerate at least 3 hours.

Remove chicken and lemon slices. Discard lemon slices; reserve marinade. Cover and grill chicken, bone sides down, 5 to 6 inches from medium coals, 15 to 20 minutes; turn chicken. Cover and grill, turning and brushing 2 or 3 times with reserved marinade, until chicken is done, 20 to 40 minutes longer. Roll edges of lemon slices in paprika; arrange around chicken.

Wine-marinated Chicken

3/4 cup dry red wine
1/4 cup lemon juice
1 tablespoon instant minced onion
1/2 teaspoon salt
1/2 teaspoon aromatic bitters
2 1/2-pound broiler-fryer chicken, cut up

Mix all ingredients except chicken pieces; pour over chicken. Cover and refrigerate at least 1 hour.

Remove chicken; reserve marinade. Cover and grill chicken, bone sides down, 5 to 6 inches from medium coals, 15 to 20 minutes; turn chicken. Cover and grill, turning and brushing 2 or 3 times with reserved marinade, until chicken is done, 20 to 40 minutes longer.

Honey-glazed Chicken

1/2 cup honey
2 tablespoons vegetable oil
2 tablespoons prepared mustard
2 tablespoons lemon juice
1/2 teaspoon grated lemon peel
1/2 teaspoon salt
2 1/2-pound broiler-fryer chicken, cut up

Mix all ingredients except chicken pieces. Cover and grill chicken, bone sides down, 5 to 6 inches from medium coals, 15 to 30 minutes; turn chicken. Cover and grill, turning and brushing 2 or 3 times with honey mixture, until chicken is done, 20 to 40 minutes longer.

Fiery Chicken

3/4 cup tomato and yellow chili sauce
    with onions
1 to 2 teaspoons chopped hot or mild
    green chilies
1 tablespoon chili powder
1 tablespoon vegetable oil
2 1/2-pound broiler-fryer chicken, cut into
    quarters

Mix all ingredients except chicken quarters. Cover and grill chicken, bone sides down, 5 to 6 inches from medium coals, 20 to 35 minutes; turn and brush chicken with chili sauce mixture. Cover and grill, turning and brushing 2 or 3 times with chili sauce mixture, until chicken is done, 25 to 45 minutes longer. Cut into serving pieces.

Chicken Afghanistan

3/4 cup plain yogurt
2 tablespoons lemon juice
1 tablespoon vegetable oil
1 teaspoon salt
1 clove garlic, crushed
1 teaspoon ground cumin
1 teaspoon ground ginger
1 teaspoon paprika
1 teaspoon almond extract
2 1/2-pound broiler-fryer chicken, cut up
1 lemon, thinly sliced
Paprika

Mix yogurt, lemon juice, oil, salt, garlic, cumin, ginger, 1 teaspoon paprika and the almond extract; pour over chicken pieces. Cover and refrigerate at least 1 hour.

Remove chicken; reserve marinade. Cover and grill chicken, bone sides down, 5 to 6 inches from medium coals, 15 to 30 minutes; turn chicken. Cover and grill, turning and brushing 2 or 3 times with reserved marinade, until chicken is done, 20 to 40 minutes longer. Sprinkle lemon slices with paprika; arrange on chicken.

Oriental Chicken Wings

1/4 cup chili sauce
1/4 cup soy sauce
1/4 cup vinegar
2 tablespoons honey
1 tablespoon vegetable oil
2 teaspoons chili powder
1/2 teaspoon garlic powder
18 chicken wings (3 to 4 pounds)

Mix all ingredients except chicken wings, pour over chicken. Cover and refrigerate at least 1 hour.

Remove chicken; reserve marinade. Cover and grill chicken 5 to 6 inches from medium coals, turning and brushing 2 or 3 times with reserved marinade, until chicken is done, 20 to 35 minutes.

Following pages: Honey-glazed Chicken

Chicken Legs Caribbean

8 SERVINGS

¹⁄₄ cup dark rum
1 tablespoon chili powder
1 tablespoon molasses
¹⁄₄ teaspoon red pepper sauce
4 chicken drumsticks
4 chicken thighs
Grilled Pineapple (below)

Mix all ingredients except chicken pieces and Grilled Pineapple; pour over chicken. Cover and refrigerate at least 1 hour.

Remove chicken; reserve marinade. Cover and grill chicken, bone sides down, 5 to 6 inches from medium coals, 15 to 20 minutes; turn chicken. Cover and grill, turning and brushing 2 or 3 times with reserved marinade, until chicken is done, 20 to 40 minutes longer. Serve with Grilled Pineapple.

GRILLED PINEAPPLE

1 medium-size ripe pineapple
¹⁄₄ cup honey

Cut off top of pineapple. Cut pineapple lengthwise into 6 wedges; cut off pineapple core. Loosen fruit by slicing from rind (do not remove rind). Drizzle honey over fruit; let stand 1 hour.

Grill pineapple, rind side down, 5 to 6 inches from medium coals until heated through, 20 to 25 minutes.

Chicken Breasts Paprika

¼ *cup margarine or butter, softened*
1 tablespoon paprika
1 teaspoon salt
¼ *teaspoon pepper*
2 cloves garlic, crushed
*3 whole chicken breasts (about 2
pounds), cut into halves*

Mix all ingredients except chicken breasts. Cover and grill chicken, bone sides down, 5 to 6 inches from medium coals, 10 to 20 minutes; turn chicken. Cover and grill, turning and brushing 2 or 3 times with margarine mixture, until chicken is done, 25 to 35 minutes longer.

Chicken Breasts Teriyaki

¼ *cup soy sauce*
¼ *cup sweet white wine*
1 tablespoon sugar
1 tablespoon vegetable oil
1 teaspoon crushed gingerroot or ¼
teaspoon ground ginger
1 clove garlic, crushed
*2 whole chicken breasts (about 1*½
*pounds), boned, skinned and cut into
halves*

Mix all ingredients except chicken breasts; pour over chicken. Cover and refrigerate at least 1 hour.

Remove chicken; reserve marinade. Cover and grill chicken 5 to 6 inches from medium coals, 10 to 20 minutes; turn chicken. Cover and grill, turning and brushing 2 or 3 times with reserved marinade, until chicken is done, 10 to 20 minutes longer.

Rotisserie Cornish Hens

3 frozen Rock Cornish hens (about 1¼
  pounds each), thawed
1 teaspoon salt
1 can (6 ounces) frozen orange juice
  concentrate, thawed
¼ cup catsup
2 tablespoons soy sauce
½ teaspoon dried tarragon leaves

Rub cavities of hens with salt. Flatten hen wings over breasts; tie with heavy string to hold securely. Tie legs together, then tie to tails. Insert spit rod through cavities of hens from breast ends toward tails; hold firmly in place with adjustable holding forks. Mix remaining ingredients.

Cover and cook hens on rotisserie about 4 inches from low heat until done (leg bones move easily), 1¼ to 2 hours; brush hens 2 or 3 times with orange juice mixture during last 10 minutes of cooking. Heat remaining orange juice mixture until warm. Cut hens lengthwise into halves. Serve with orange juice mixture.

Wine-basted Hens

6 SERVINGS

3 frozen Rock Cornish hens (about 1¼
  pounds each), thawed
1 teaspoon salt
¼ cup red currant jelly
¼ cup dry red wine
1 tablespoon margarine or butter
½ teaspoon garlic powder

Cut hens lengthwise into halves; rub cut sides with salt. Heat remaining ingredients over medium heat, stirring constantly, until jelly is melted.

Cover and grill hens, bone sides down, 5 to 6 inches from medium coals, 20 to 35 minutes; turn hens. Cover and grill, turning and brushing 2 or 3 times with jelly mixture, until hens are done, 25 to 35 minutes longer. Serve with any remaining jelly mixture.

Chicken, Italian Style

4 SERVINGS

8 chicken drumsticks, thighs or breast
   halves
1 teaspoon salt
4 medium potatoes, pared and cut
   lengthwise into 1/4-inch slices
4 medium zucchini, cut into 1/4-inch
   slices
Salt
12 large pitted ripe olives
1 can (8 ounces) tomato sauce
1 teaspoon dried oregano leaves
4 tablespoons margarine or butter

Sprinkle chicken pieces with 1 teaspoon salt. Layer potatoes, zucchini and salt on a double layer of 18 × 12-inch heavy-duty aluminum foil. Top with chicken, olives, tomato sauce and oregano; dot with margarine. Wrap securely in foil.

Cook on grill 5 inches from medium coals, 12 to 15 minutes; turn once. Grill until chicken is done, 12 to 15 minutes longer.

Garlic Chicken on the Rotisserie

6 SERVINGS

2 tablespoons lemon juice
2 tablespoons vegetable oil
1 teaspoon dried oregano leaves
1/2 teaspoon garlic powder
5 cloves garlic, crushed
1/2 teaspoon salt
2 1/2-pound broiler-fryer chicken

Mix lemon juice, oil, oregano and garlic powder; reserve. Mix garlic and salt; rub cavity of chicken with salt mixture. Flatten chicken wings over breast; tie with heavy string to hold securely. Tie legs together, then tie to tail. Insert spit rod through cavity of chicken from breast end toward tail; hold firmly in place with adjustable holding forks.

Cover and cook chicken on rotisserie about 4 inches from low heat until done (leg bone moves easily), 1 1/2 to 2 hours. Brush chicken 2 or 3 times with reserved lemon juice mixture during last 15 minutes of cooking. Cut into serving pieces.

Following pages: Wine-basted Hens and Grilled Corn

Turkey and Vegetable Barbecue

10 TO 12 SERVINGS

8- to 10-pound turkey
2 teaspoons salt
1/4 teaspoon cayenne pepper
2 onions, cut into fourths
Vegetable oil
Thyme Butter (below)
Roasted Potatoes (below)
Roasted Corn (below)
Grilled Tomatoes (see page 61)

Rub cavity of turkey with salt and cayenne pepper; place onions in cavity. Fold wings across back with tips touching. Tie legs together with heavy string, then tie to tail. Brush turkey with oil. Insert barbecue meat thermometer so tip is in thickest part of inside thigh muscle and does not touch bone.

Arrange hot coals around edge of fire box; place foil drip pan under grilling area. Cover and grill turkey, breast side up, 5 to 6 inches from drip pan, brushing occasionally with Thyme Butter, until breast meat is white when pierced with knife (185°), 3 to 4 hours. Add potatoes, corn and tomatoes as directed below. Add coals during cooking to maintain even heat. Let turkey stand 15 minutes before carving. Serve with Roasted Potatoes, Roasted Corn and Grilled Tomatoes.

THYME BUTTER

2 tablespoons margarine or butter,
  softened
1/2 teaspoon ground thyme

Mix margarine and ground thyme.

ROASTED POTATOES

Baking potatoes
Margarine or butter, softened

Rub baking potatoes with margarine. Place on cooking grill. Cover and grill, turning once, until tender, 1 to 1 1/2 hours.

ROASTED CORN

Corn in its husk
Margarine or butter, softened

Husk ears of corn and remove silk. Rub corn with margarine. Place on cooking grill. Cover and grill until tender, 25 to 35 minutes.

GRILLED TOMATOES

Tomatoes
Grated Parmesan cheese
Margarine or butter

Cut thin slice from stem ends of tomatoes. Sprinkle tomatoes with cheese; dot with margarine. Place tomatoes on cooking grill. Cover and grill until heated through, 10 to 15 minutes.

Savory Duckling

Coriander Sauce (below)
5-pound ready-to-cook duckling
2 teaspoons salt
1 small onion
3 sprigs parsley

Prepare Coriander Sauce. Rub cavity of duckling with salt; place onion and parsley in cavity. Fasten neck skin of duckling to back with skewer. Flatten wings over breast; tie with heavy string to hold securely. Tie legs together, then tie to tail. Insert spit rod through cavity of duckling from breast end toward tail; hold firmly in place with adjustable holding forks. Insert 1/4 cup of the sauce into cavity of duckling; use additional skewers to keep cavity closed securely.

Arrange medium-hot coals at back of firebox; place foil drip pan under grilling area. Cook duckling on rotisserie until done, 2 hours; prick skin with a fork frequently to drain away excess fat. Brush duckling with sauce 3 or 4 times during last 20 minutes of cooking.

CORIANDER SAUCE

1/2 cup dry vermouth or apple juice
1/2 cup dark corn syrup
1 tablespoon lemon juice
1 teaspoon ground coriander

Mix all ingredients in saucepan. Simmer uncovered until mixture is reduced by half, 15 to 20 minutes.

Following pages: Savory Duckling and Stuffed Acorn Squash

· 4 ·

FISH AND SEAFOOD

Sole in Foil

1 pound sole fillets
1/2 teaspoon salt
1/2 cup thinly sliced fresh mushrooms
2 tablespoons margarine or butter
1 cup dry white wine
2 teaspoons instant minced onion
1 tablespoon cornstarch
1/3 cup cold water
2 tablespoons lemon juice
6 ounces cleaned raw shrimp
1 tablespoon snipped parsley

Cut fish fillets into 6 serving pieces; sprinkle with salt. Cook and stir mushrooms in margarine until tender. Add wine and onion. Mix cornstarch and water; stir into wine mixture. Cook, stirring constantly, until mixture thickens and boils; boil and stir 1 minute. Stir in lemon juice.

Place each piece fish on a double layer of 14 × 9-inch piece of heavy-duty aluminum foil; top each with 1 ounce shrimp. Turn foil up around fish; pour sauce over shrimp. Sprinkle each with 1/2 teaspoon parsley. Wrap securely in foil. Grill about 4 inches from medium coals, turning once, until fish flakes easily with fork, 20 to 25 minutes.

Teriyaki Fillets

1 1/2 pounds cod, haddock or halibut
  fillets, about 1 inch thick
1/4 cup lemon juice
2 tablespoons soy sauce
1 tablespoon vegetable oil
2 cloves garlic, crushed

If fish fillets are large, cut into 8 serving pieces. Mix all ingredients except fish; pour over fish. Cover and refrigerate at least 1 hour.

Remove fish; reserve marinade. Cover and grill fish about 4 inches from medium coals, turning once and brushing occasionally with reserved marinade, until fish flakes easily with fork, 12 to 20 minutes. Garnish with lemon wedges and parsley sprigs, if desired.

Lime Fish Fillets

2 pounds fish fillets (bass, pike, mackerel
  or trout)
Vegetable oil
Paprika
1/2 cup margarine or butter, melted
1/4 cup lime juice
Salt and pepper
Lime wedges

Brush fish with vegetable oil; sprinkle with paprika. Place fish in well-greased hinged wire basket or on well-greased grill 3 to 4 inches from medium coals. Cook, turning once, and brushing frequently with mixture of margarine and lime juice, until fish flakes easily with fork, 5 to 7 minutes. Sprinkle with salt and pepper; serve with lime wedges.

BACON-WRAPPED FISH FILLETS: Before grilling fish, place lime slices on side of fish; wrap fish and lime slices with bacon slices. Secure bacon with wooden picks.

Following pages: Lime Fish Fillet

MINT

ilis 'Variegata'

SWEET CECILY

Myrrhis odorata

Dilled Cod

1/4 cup lemon juice
1 tablespoon vegetable oil
1/2 teaspoon dried dill weed
1/2 teaspoon onion powder
1/2 teaspoon paprika
1/2 teaspoon salt
1/8 teaspoon red pepper sauce
1 package (12 ounces) frozen cod
    portions, thawed

Mix all ingredients except fish portions; pour over fish. Let stand uncovered 15 minutes.

Remove fish; reserve marinade. Cover and grill fish about 4 inches from medium coals, turning once and brushing occasionally with reserved marinade, until fish flakes easily with fork, 12 to 20 minutes. Garnish with fresh dill weed and lemon wedges, if desired.

Confetti Fish in Foil

2 slices bacon, cut into 1/2-inch pieces
3 green onions (with tops), cut into
    3/4-inch pieces
1 green pepper, cut into 3/4-inch pieces
1 stalk celery, cut into 3/4-inch pieces
1 medium tomato, cut into 3/4-inch pieces
1/2 teaspoon salt
1/8 teaspoon pepper
1 package (14 ounces) frozen pike fillets,
    thawed
1 tablespoon plus 1 teaspoon lemon juice

Cook and stir bacon, onions, green pepper and celery until vegetables are crisp-tender, 3 to 5 minutes. Stir in tomato, salt and pepper; remove from heat. Divide fish fillets among four 12-inch squares of heavy-duty aluminum foil. Sprinkle each fillet with 1 teaspoon lemon juice; top each with about 1/2 cup bacon-vegetable mixture. Wrap securely in foil.

Grill packets about 4 inches from hot coals, turning once, until fish flakes easily with fork, 20 to 30 minutes.

Mediterranean Snapper

6 SERVINGS

1/2 cup spaghetti sauce
2 tablespoons lime juice
1 teaspoon dried oregano leaves
1/2 teaspoon salt
1 or 2 cloves garlic, crushed
1 1/2 pounds red snapper fillets, 1/2 to 3/4
    inch thick

Mix all ingredients except fish fillets; pour over fish. Cover and refrigerate at least 1 hour.

Remove fish; reserve marinade. Cover and grill fish about 4 inches from medium coals, turning once and brushing 2 or 3 times with reserved marinade, until fish flakes easily with fork, 15 to 25 minutes. Cut into serving pieces. Garnish with lime wedges and watercress, if desired.

Red Snapper Fillets with Flavored Butters

6 SERVINGS

1 1/2 pounds red snapper or cod fillets, 1/4
    to 1/2 inch thick
Lemon Butter or Mustard Butter (below)

Cut red snapper fillets into 6 serving pieces. Cover and grill fish about 4 inches from medium coals, turning and brushing occasionally with one of the flavored butters, until fish flakes easily with fork, 15 to 25 minutes. Cut into serving pieces.

LEMON BUTTER

2 tablespoons butter or margarine,
    melted
1 tablespoon lemon juice
1/2 teaspoon grated lemon peel
1/2 teaspoon Worcestershire sauce

Mix all ingredients.

MUSTARD BUTTER

2 tablespoons butter or margarine,
    softened
1 1/2 teaspoons dry mustard
1/2 teaspoon lemon pepper

Mix all ingredients.

Monterey Fish Steaks

6 SERVINGS

1 1/2 pounds swordfish, halibut or salmon steaks, 3/4 to 1 inch thick
1 teaspoon salt
1/4 teaspoon pepper
1/4 cup margarine or butter, melted
1 tablespoon lemon juice
1 teaspoon dried chervil leaves
Avocado Sauce or Caper Sauce (below)
Lemon wedges

Sprinkle fish steaks with salt and pepper. Mix margarine, lemon juice and chervil. Cover and grill fish about 4 inches from medium coals, turning once and brushing 2 or 3 times with margarine mixture, until fish flakes easily with fork, 15 to 25 minutes. Cut into serving pieces. Serve with Avocado Sauce or Caper Sauce and lemon wedges.

AVOCADO SAUCE

1 small avocado, cut up
1/3 cup dairy sour cream
1 teaspoon lemon juice
1/4 teaspoon salt
Few drops red pepper sauce

Beat all ingredients with hand beater until smooth.

CAPER SAUCE

1 lemon
1/4 cup capers
1 tablespoon margarine or butter
1 tablespoon snipped parsley
1/4 teaspoon salt

Pare and chop lemon, removing seeds and membrane; mix with remaining ingredients. Heat until hot.

Grilled Breaded Fish

2 TO 4 SERVINGS

FISH FILLETS

1 package (8, 12 or 20 ounces) frozen extra crispy batter-dipped cod, flounder, haddock or perch fillets

Place fillets on greased grill. Cover and grill about 4 inches from coals until hot, 5 to 8 minutes on each side for 8-ounce package, 6 to 9 minutes for 12- and 20-ounce packages.

FISH STICKS

1 package (8 ounces) frozen extra crispy batter-dipped fish sticks

Place fish sticks on greased grill. Cover and grill about 4 inches from coals until hot, 5 minutes on each side.

Note: If using a partial package of fish fillets or sticks, adjust time accordingly.

Fish Steaks with Chives and Lemon

6 SERVINGS

1/4 cup lemon juice
3 tablespoons snipped chives
2 tablespoons vegetable oil
1 teaspoon dried dill weed
1 teaspoon paprika
1/2 teaspoon salt
1 1/2 pounds halibut, salmon or swordfish steaks, 3/4 to 1 inch thick

Mix all ingredients except fish steaks; pour over fish. Cover and refrigerate at least 1 hour.

Remove fish; reserve marinade. Cover and grill fish about 4 inches from medium coals, turning once and brushing 2 or 3 times with reserved marinade, until fish flakes easily with fork, 10 to 15 minutes. Cut into serving pieces. Garnish with thin cucumber slices, if desired.

Smoked Salmon

6 SERVINGS

2 limes, thinly sliced
1 lemon, thinly sliced
3 pounds salmon steaks, 1 inch thick
1/2 cup margarine or butter, melted
1 teaspoon curry powder
1/2 teaspoon salt
1/4 teaspoon pepper

Soak 3 cups wood chips in water about 30 minutes. Form an 18-inch square pan from a double layer of heavy-duty aluminum foil. Arrange lime and lemon slices in pan; place fish on slices. Mix margarine and curry powder; pour over fish. Sprinkle with salt and pepper. Arrange hot coals around edge of firebox. Drain chips; add to hot coals. Place foil pan on grill about 4 inches from coals; cover and grill until fish flakes easily with fork, 40 to 50 minutes.

Following pages: Monterey Fish Steaks and Avocado Sauce

Fish and Vegetables

8- to 10-pound salmon, cod or lake trout,
  cleaned
Salt
Pepper
Garden Vegetable Stuffing (below)
½ cup margarine or butter, melted
¼ cup lemon juice
Vegetable oil

Sprinkle cavity of fish with salt and pepper; spoon Garden Vegetable Stuffing into cavity. Secure with skewers and lace with string.

Mix margarine and lemon juice; reserve. Brush fish with oil; place in hinged wire grill basket. Cover and grill about 4 inches from medium coals, turning basket 3 times and brushing fish occasionally with reserved lemon juice mixture, until fish flakes easily with fork, 45 to 60 minutes. Cut into serving pieces.

GARDEN VEGETABLE STUFFING

1 large onion, finely chopped (about 1
  cup)
¼ cup margarine or butter
2 cups dry bread cubes
1 cup coarsely shredded carrot
1 cup cut-up mushrooms
1 tablespoon plus 1½ teaspoons lemon
  juice
1 egg
1 clove garlic, finely chopped
2 teaspoons salt
¼ teaspoon dried marjoram leaves
¼ teaspoon pepper

Cook and stir onion in margarine until onion is tender; toss with remaining ingredients.

Rice-stuffed Fish

6 SERVINGS

3 cups cooked rice
½ cup mayonnaise or salad dressing
½ cup finely chopped water chestnuts
⅓ cup chopped green onions (with tops)
1 jar (2 ounces) chopped pimiento,
*   drained*
¾ teaspoon salt
¼ teaspoon pepper
3 pounds whitefish or bass (1 or 2 whole
*   fish), cleaned*
Margarine or butter, melted

Mix all ingredients except fish and margarine; spoon into fish cavity. Secure with skewers and lace with string.

Place fish in lightly greased hinged wire grill basket. Cover and grill about 4 inches from medium coals, turning basket once and brushing fish 3 or 4 times with margarine, until fish flakes easily with fork, 30 to 40 minutes. Cut into serving pieces. Garnish with lemon wedges, if desired.

Note: Extra stuffing can be heated 30 minutes in covered aluminum foil pan on side of grill.

Crab-stuffed Rainbow Trout

12 SERVINGS

6 rainbow trout (8 ounces each dressed
*   weight)*
Salt
1 can (7¾ ounces) crabmeat, drained
*   and cartilage removed*
½ cup finely chopped water chestnuts
¼ cup dry bread crumbs
¼ cup mayonnaise or salad dressing
½ teaspoon crushed tarragon leaves
¼ cup margarine or butter, melted
1 tablespoon lemon juice

Sprinkle cavities of fish lightly with salt. Mix crabmeat, water chestnuts, bread crumbs, mayonnaise and tarragon; toss. Spoon into fish cavities; secure with skewers if necessary.

Mix margarine and lemon juice; reserve. Place fish in well-greased hinged wire grill basket. Cover and grill about 4 inches from medium coals, turning basket once and brushing fish frequently with reserved lemon juice mixture, until fish flakes easily with fork, 16 to 20 minutes. Cut into serving pieces.

Garlic Shrimp

12 TO 18 SERVINGS

½ cup margarine or butter
2 teaspoons garlic salt
⅛ teaspoon red pepper sauce
3 pounds cleaned raw shrimp
*1 can (8 ounces) sliced water chestnuts,
  drained*
1 large green pepper, cut into rings
1 tablespoon finely chopped onion
½ teaspoon salt
½ teaspoon dried tarragon leaves

Form a pan, 11 × 11 × ½ inch, from a double layer of heavy-duty aluminum foil. Place margarine, garlic salt and pepper sauce in pan; place on grill 4 to 6 inches from medium coals until margarine is melted. Remove pan from grill; add remaining ingredients. Cover pan with piece of heavy-duty aluminum foil, sealing edges well. Grill until shrimp is done, 20 to 30 minutes.

Grilled Butterflied Shrimp

6 SERVINGS

*1 pound fresh raw shrimp (18 to 20 in
  shells)*
½ cup dry white wine
1 tablespoon snipped parsley
1 tablespoon vegetable oil
1 teaspoon dried basil leaves
½ teaspoon salt
1 bay leaf, crushed
½ lemon, thinly sliced

Peel shrimp. Make a shallow cut lengthwise down back of each shrimp; wash out sand vein. Press each shrimp flat into butterfly shape. Mix remaining ingredients; pour over shrimp. Cover and refrigerate at least 1 hour.

Remove shrimp; reserve marinade. Arrange shrimp in lightly greased hinged wire grill basket. Cover and grill about 4 inches from medium coals, turning basket and brushing shrimp 2 or 3 times with reserved marinade, until shrimp is pink, 6 to 10 minutes. Garnish with lemon slices and, if desired, parsley.

Scallop Kabobs

1 pound fresh or frozen scallops
2 tablespoons snipped parsley
2 tablespoons vegetable oil
2 tablespoons soy sauce
2 tablespoons lemon juice
½ teaspoon salt
Dash of pepper
1 can (4 ounces) whole mushrooms,
*   drained*
12 slices bacon
1 can (13¼ ounces) pineapple chunks,
*   drained*

Thaw scallops if frozen. Mix parsley, oil, soy sauce, lemon juice, salt and pepper; pour over scallops and mushrooms. Cover and refrigerate, turning scallops and mushrooms once, at least 30 minutes.

Remove scallops and mushrooms; reserve marinade. Partially fry bacon (just until it begins to curl); drain and cut slices into halves. Alternate scallops, mushrooms, bacon and pineapple chunks on each of 6 metal skewers. Cover and grill kabobs about 4 inches from medium coals, turning and brushing 2 or 3 times with reserved marinade, until scallops flake easily with fork, 12 to 20 minutes.

Grilled Lobster Tails

6 medium fresh or frozen lobster tails
½ cup margarine or butter, melted
⅓ cup lemon juice
2 teaspoons Worcestershire sauce
½ teaspoon onion salt
½ cup margarine or butter, melted
Lemon wedges

Thaw lobster tails if frozen; cut away thin undershell (covering meat of lobster tails) with kitchen scissors. To prevent tail from curling, bend each tail backward toward shell; crack. Mix ½ cup margarine, the lemon juice, Worcestershire sauce and onion salt.

Cover and grill lobster tails, shell sides down, about 4 inches from medium coals, 10 minutes, brushing 4 to 6 times with margarine mixture; turn lobster tails. Cover and grill until meat is opaque, 5 to 10 minutes longer. Serve with remaining ½ cup margarine and the lemon wedges.

Following pages: Grilled Butterflied Shrimp

· 5 ·

VEGETABLES

Vegetable Kabobs

1 1/2 pounds zucchini (about 3 medium),
cut into 3/4-inch slices
2 green peppers, cut into 1 1/2-inch pieces
18 cherry tomatoes
18 whole mushrooms
1/2 cup Italian dressing
1 teaspoon garlic salt

Alternate vegetables on each of 6 metal skewers, leaving space between vegetables. Mix dressing and garlic salt; brush on vegetables.

Cover and grill kabobs 5 to 6 inches from medium coals, turning and brushing 2 or 3 times with dressing mixture, until vegetables are crisp-tender, 10 to 15 minutes.

SMOKY VEGETABLE KABOBS: Cover 1 cup hickory chips with water. Let stand 30 minutes; drain. Add hickory chips to hot coals. Continue as directed.

Mushrooms Lyonnaise

2 tablespoons instant minced onion
1/4 cup water
1 pound fresh mushrooms, sliced
2 tablespoons snipped parsley
1/2 teaspoon salt
1/4 teaspoon pepper
1/4 cup margarine or butter

Mix onion and water. Place mushrooms on a square double layer of 18-inch heavy-duty aluminum foil. Sprinkle with onion mixture, parsley, salt and pepper; dot with margarine. Wrap securely in foil. Cover and grill packet 5 to 6 inches from medium coals, turning 2 or 3 times, until mushrooms are done, 15 to 20 minutes.

Onion and Carrot Kabobs

6 SERVINGS

10 medium yellow onions, peeled
6 large carrots, each scraped and cut
  into thirds
¼ cup molasses
2 tablespoons prepared mustard
1 tablespoon vinegar

Heat several inches salted water (½ teaspoon salt to 1 cup water) to boiling. Add onions and carrots. Cover and heat to boiling. Cook until crisp-tender, 10 to 15 minutes; drain. Mix molasses, mustard and vinegar. Alternate onions and carrots on each of 4 metal skewers, leaving space between vegetables. Brush vegetables with molasses mixture. Cover and grill kabobs 5 to 6 inches from medium coals, turning and brushing 2 or 3 times with molasses mixture, until tender, 10 to 15 minutes.

Grilled Corn

Corn in its husk
Margarine or butter, softened
Salt
Pepper
2 tablespoons water

For each serving, husk corn and remove silk. Spread margarine on corn; place each ear corn on double thickness of heavy-duty aluminum foil. Sprinkle with salt, pepper and water. Wrap securely in foil; twist ends of foil. Place corn on medium coals. Cover and cook, turning once, until done, 10 to 15 minutes.

CORN IN THE HUSK: For each serving, remove large outer husks; turn back inner husks and remove silk. Spread margarine on corn. Pull husks back over ears, tying with fine wire. Grill corn 3 inches from medium coals, turning frequently until done, 20 to 30 minutes.

Lemon Potatoes

4 large potatoes, pared and cubed
¼ cup margarine or butter, melted
¼ cup lemon juice
2 teaspoons salt
1 teaspoon grated lemon peel
¼ teaspoon ground nutmeg
¼ teaspoon coarsely ground pepper
1 green onion (with top), chopped

Cook potato cubes in boiling salted water just until tender. Mix remaining ingredients; toss gently with potatoes. Spoon potato mixture onto a double layer of 20 × 14-inch piece heavy-duty aluminum foil. Wrap securely in foil. Let stand at room temperature 1 hour. Grill 4 inches from medium coals, turning once, 30 minutes.

Grilled German Potato Salad

5 medium potatoes (about 1½ pounds)
8 slices bacon, crisply fried and crumbled
1 cup finely chopped celery
3 green onions (with tops), finely
  chopped
½ cup mayonnaise or salad dressing
¼ cup white vinegar
2 teaspoons sugar
1 teaspoon salt
1 teaspoon dry mustard
¼ teaspoon coarsely ground pepper

Heat 1 inch salted water (½ teaspoon salt to 1 cup water) to boiling. Add potatoes. Heat to boiling; reduce heat. Cover and cook until tender, 20 to 30 minutes. Drain and cool. Cut potatoes into cubes. Mix potatoes, bacon, celery and onions. Mix remaining ingredients. Pour over potato mixture; toss. Place mixture on a double layer of 18 × 13-inch piece of heavy-duty aluminum foil; wrap securely. Cover and grill packet 5 to 6 inches from medium coals, turning 2 or 3 times, until done, 20 to 30 minutes.

Stuffed Acorn Squash

6 SERVINGS

3 medium acorn squash, cut into halves
4 1/2 cups chopped apple
3/4 cup chopped walnuts
1/4 cup packed brown sugar
1/4 cup plus 2 tablespoons margarine or
    butter

Remove seeds and fibers from squash. Place each squash half on a double layer of heavy-duty aluminum foil. Place 3/4 cup chopped apple, 2 tablespoons chopped walnuts and 2 teaspoons brown sugar in each half. Top each with 1 tablespoon margarine. Wrap securely in foil. Cover and grill 3 to 5 inches from medium coals, turning once, until tender, about 1 hour.

Italian-style Zucchini

6 SERVINGS

1/4 cup vegetable oil
2 tablespoons vinegar
1 teaspoon dried oregano leaves
1 teaspoon salt
1/2 teaspoon garlic powder
2 pounds zucchini (about 6 small)

Mix all ingredients except zucchini. Cut zucchini lengthwise into halves; dip in oil mixture, coating all sides. Arrange zucchini in hinged wire grill basket. Cover and grill 5 to 6 inches from medium coals, turning basket 2 or 3 times and brushing zucchini 2 or 3 times with oil mixture, until tender, 12 to 18 minutes.

Grilled Eggplant

8 SERVINGS

1/3 cup vegetable oil
2 tablespoons lemon juice
2 cloves garlic, crushed
2 teaspoons dried oregano leaves, crushed
1 teaspoon salt
2 medium eggplants (about 2 1/2 pounds)
1 cup shredded mozzarella cheese (about
    4 ounces)

Mix all ingredients except eggplants and cheese. Cut eggplants into 1 1/2-inch slices; dip in oil mixture, coating both sides. Cover and grill eggplants 5 to 6 inches from medium coals until tender, 8 to 12 minutes; turn and brush eggplants 2 or 3 times with oil mixture and top with cheese during last 2 minutes of grilling.

· 6 ·

BREADS AND DESSERTS

Sesame Bread

2 cups variety baking mix
1/4 cup sesame seed
1/2 teaspoon salt
1/2 cup cold water

Stir baking mix, sesame seed, salt and water to a soft dough. Gently smooth dough into a ball on floured surface. Knead 5 times.

Divide dough in half. Roll or pat each half into a rectangle, 12 × 8 inches; cut lengthwise in half.

Grill flat bread 5 inches from medium coals, turning once, 6 to 8 minutes. Cut each strip into 4 pieces.

Parmesan Slices

6 SERVINGS

1/2 cup grated Parmesan cheese
1/4 cup margarine or butter, softened
6 one-inch-thick slices French or Vienna bread
1 tablespoon poppy seed

Mix cheese and margarine; spread on both sides of bread slices. Sprinkle with poppy seed. Grill bread 5 to 6 inches from medium coals, turning once, until golden brown, 6 to 8 minutes.

Barbecue Bread

1 loaf (1 pound) French or Vienna bread
Spread (below)

Cut French bread diagonally into 1-inch slices or Vienna bread into ½-inch slices, cutting almost to bottom of loaf. Spread one of the spreads between slices of bread. Place half of the slices on 14 × 18-inch piece of heavy-duty aluminum foil; wrap securely. Repeat with remaining slices. Cover and grill bread 5 to 6 inches from medium coals, turning once, until hot, 8 to 10 minutes. Open foil; grill bread uncovered 5 minutes longer.

BLUE CHEESE SPREAD

½ cup margarine or butter, softened
¼ cup crumbled blue cheese
2 tablespoons grated Parmesan cheese

Mix all ingredients.

PARMESAN CHEESE SPREAD

½ cup mayonnaise or salad dressing
¼ cup grated Parmesan cheese
1 teaspoon dried oregano leaves

Mix all ingredients.

GARLIC-CHIVE SPREAD

½ cup margarine or butter, softened
¼ cup snipped chives
1 or 2 cloves garlic, crushed

Mix all ingredients.

CREAMY PEANUT BUTTER SPREAD

1 package (3 ounces) cream cheese,
softened
3 tablespoons creamy peanut butter
1 tablespoon margarine or butter,
softened

Mix all ingredients.

GARLIC BUTTER SPREAD

1/2 cup margarine or butter, softened
1 medium clove garlic, crushed

Mix ingredients.

TARRAGON BUTTER SPREAD

1/2 cup margarine or butter, softened
1 teaspoon dried tarragon leaves
1/4 teaspoon paprika

Mix all ingredients.

ONION BUTTER SPREAD

1/2 cup margarine or butter, softened
2 tablespoons finely chopped onion or
  snipped chives

Mix ingredients.

HERB-CHEESE BUTTER SPREAD

1/2 cup margarine or butter, softened
2 teaspoons snipped parsley
1/2 teaspoon dried oregano leaves
2 tablespoons grated Parmesan cheese
1/8 teaspoon garlic salt

Mix all ingredients.

HERB-LEMON BUTTER SPREAD

1/2 cup margarine or butter, softened
2 teaspoons lemon juice
1 tablespoon snipped fresh herbs or 1
  teaspoon dried herbs
Dash of salt

Mix all ingredients.

SEEDED BUTTER

1/2 cup margarine or butter, softened
1 to 2 teaspoons celery, poppy, dill or
  sesame seed

Mix ingredients.

Apples Alfresco

For each serving:

1 baking apple
1 tablespoon packed brown sugar
2 teaspoons red cinnamon candies
2 teaspoons lemon juice
1 pineapple spear
Cinnamon Whipped Cream (below)

Wash apple; core to within ½ inch of bottom. Score skin ⅛ inch deep in petal design. Fill cavity with remaining ingredients except Cinnamon Whipped Cream. Wrap securely in a double layer of 8-inch square heavy-duty aluminum foil. Grill 4 inches from medium coals, 30 to 40 minutes or until soft. Serve with Cinnamon Whipped Cream.

CINNAMON WHIPPED CREAM

½ cup whipping cream
1 tablespoon granulated sugar
½ teaspoon ground cinnamon

Beat all ingredients until stiff.

Grilled Shortcake

6 TO 8 SERVINGS

2 ⅓ cups variety baking mix
3 tablespoons sugar
3 tablespoons margarine or butter, melted
½ cup milk
Fresh berries or mixed fruit
Sweetened whipped cream

Stir baking mix, sugar, margarine and milk to a soft dough. Spread dough in one greased 9-inch foil pie pan. Invert another greased 9-inch foil pie pan over pan with dough. Secure rims together with spring-type wooden clothespins. Grill shortcake 4 inches from hot coals, 15 minutes on each side or until brown. Serve warm with berries and whipped cream.

Following pages: Grilled Shortcake

Stringy Cheese Loaf

1 loaf (1 pound) French bread
1 package (3 ounces) cream cheese, softened
1 cup shredded mozzarella cheese (about 4 ounces)
1/4 cup chopped green onions (with tops)
2 tablespoons margarine or butter, softened
1/2 teaspoon garlic salt

Cut bread diagonally into 1-inch slices, cutting almost to bottom of loaf. Mix remaining ingredients; spread between slices of bread. Place bread on 28 × 18-inch piece of heavy-duty aluminum foil; wrap securely. Cover and grill bread 5 to 6 inches from medium coals, turning once, until cheese is melted, 8 to 10 minutes. Unwrap foil; grill bread uncovered 5 minutes longer.

Zucchini-Nut Cake

1/3 cup sliced almonds
1 cup variety baking mix
1/3 cup sugar
1/2 teaspoon ground cinnamon
1/2 cup shredded zucchini
2 tablespoons milk
1 egg
Almond Glaze (below)

Grease 8 3/4-inch foil pan; coat bottom and sides with almonds. Beat remaining ingredients, except Almond Glaze, 3 strokes.

Pour into pan. Cover with greased sheet of heavy-duty aluminum foil; secure foil to pan with spring-type wooden clothespins. Grill cake over medium coals until edges are set, about 10 minutes. Invert pan; grill until cake springs back when touched lightly, about 5 minutes longer. Remove foil and cool slightly; invert onto serving plate. Drizzle Almond Glaze over cake.

ALMOND GLAZE

1/2 cup powdered sugar
1/4 teaspoon almond extract
2 to 3 teaspoons milk.

Mix all ingredients until smooth.

· 7 ·

BARBECUE SAUCES

Sauce Parisian

1 CUP

½ cup vegetable oil
½ cup vermouth or dry white wine
1 teaspoon garlic salt
1 teaspoon onion salt

Heat all ingredients to boiling. Brush on chicken during last half of cooking period.

Lemon Sauce

1 CUP

½ cup margarine or butter
½ clove garlic, crushed
2 teaspoons all-purpose flour
⅓ cup water
3 tablespoons lemon juice
1½ teaspoons sugar
1 teaspoon salt
⅛ teaspoon pepper
⅛ teaspoon poultry seasoning
⅛ teaspoon red pepper sauce

Heat margarine in small saucepan until melted. Add garlic; cook and stir a few minutes. Stir in flour; cook over low heat, stirring until mixture is bubbly. Remove from heat. Add remaining ingredients; cook over medium heat, stirring constantly, until mixture thickens and boils. Cool and refrigerate. Brush on chicken or fish during last half of cooking period.

Texas Barbecue Sauce

2 1/4 CUPS

1 cup tomato juice
1/2 cup water
1/4 cup catsup
1/4 cup vinegar
2 tablespoons Worcestershire sauce
2 tablespoons packed brown sugar
1 tablespoon paprika
1 teaspoon dry mustard
1 teaspoon salt
1/4 teaspoon chili powder
1/8 teaspoon cayenne pepper

Mix all ingredients in small saucepan. Heat to boiling; reduce heat. Simmer uncovered until slightly thickened, about 15 minutes. Brush on chicken or pork during last half of cooking period.

Honey-Mustard Sauce

3/4 CUP

1/2 cup honey
2 tablespoons vegetable oil
2 tablespoons prepared mustard
2 tablespoons lemon juice
1/2 teaspoon grated lemon peel
1/2 teaspoon salt

Mix all ingredients. Brush on chicken 2 or 3 times during last half of cooking period.

Chef's Special Sauce

1/2 CUP

1/4 cup prepared mustard
1/4 cup pineapple juice
2 tablespoons packed brown sugar
1/2 teaspoon prepared horseradish
Dash of salt

Mix all ingredients. Heat in saucepan on grill; brush on pork or ham during last 15 minutes of cooking. Serve remaining sauce with meat.

Honey-Herb Sauce

¹/₂ cup prepared mustard
¹/₂ cup honey
1 teaspoon salt
¹/₂ teaspoon dried rosemary leaves
¹/₄ teaspoon pepper

Mix all ingredients. Brush on lamb chops, pork chops or ham during last 15 minutes of cooking. Serve remaining sauce with meat.

Orange Sauce

¹/₃ cup orange marmalade
¹/₄ cup lemon juice
¹/₄ cup soy sauce
1 clove garlic, finely chopped
2 teaspoons cornstarch
2 tablespoons water

Mix all ingredients except cornstarch and water in saucepan. Mix cornstarch and water until smooth; stir into marmalade mixture. Heat, stirring constantly, until mixture thickens and boils. Brush on pork during last 15 minutes of cooking.

Herb-Wine Sauce

¹/₄ cup dry red wine
¹/₄ cup chili sauce
¹/₄ teaspoon dried oregano leaves
¹/₄ teaspoon dried thyme leaves
¹/₄ teaspoon dried rosemary leaves

Mix all ingredients. Brush on lamb or beef during last 15 minutes of cooking.

Smoky Sauce

1 teaspoon packed brown sugar
¾ teaspoon salt
½ teaspoon prepared mustard
¼ teaspoon pepper
¼ cup water
2 tablespoons vinegar
2 tablespoons margarine or butter
1 thin slice lemon
1 slice onion
¼ cup catsup
1 tablespoon Worcestershire sauce
¾ teaspoon liquid smoke

Mix all ingredients except catsup, Worcestershire sauce and liquid smoke in small saucepan. Heat to boiling. Reduce heat and simmer uncovered 20 minutes; strain. Stir in remaining ingredients. Heat to boiling. Baste beef during last half of grilling period.

Easy Barbecue Sauce

2 tablespoons Worcestershire sauce
2 tablespoons vinegar
1 tablespoon margarine or butter, melted
⅛ teaspoon red pepper sauce

Mix all ingredients; brush on both sides of hamburgers or steaks; let stand 15 minutes. While grilling, brush meat with sauce.

Barbecue Sauce

¼ cup catsup
3 tablespoons packed brown sugar
1 teaspoon dry mustard
¼ teaspoon ground nutmeg

Mix all ingredients. Brush on during last 10 minutes of grilling period.

Note: A quick-basting or serve-with sauce prepared from readily available ingredients and made especially for hamburgers.

Zippy Horseradish Sauce

½ cup mayonnaise or salad dressing
¼ cup dairy sour cream
2 tablespoons prepared horseradish, well
  drained
2 tablespoons snipped parsley
½ teaspoon salt

Mix all ingredients; cover and refrigerate at least 1 hour.

Note: A zesty serve-with sauce for beef.

Cucumber Sauce

1 cup finely chopped unpared cucumber
  (about 1 medium)
½ teaspoon finely chopped onion
1 tablespoon prepared mustard
½ cup mayonnaise or salad dressing
½ teaspoon salt
¼ teaspoon pepper

Mix all ingredients. Cover and refrigerate.

Note: A refreshing serve-with sauce for grilled fish or shrimp.

Cocktail Sauce

1 cup catsup
1 tablespoon finely chopped onion
1 tablespoon prepared horseradish
1 teaspoon Worcestershire sauce
½ teaspoon salt
3 drops red pepper sauce

Mix all ingredients. Refrigerate at least 1 hour.

Note: A zippy serve-with sauce for any type of fish.

Parmesan Butter

2 tablespoons margarine or butter, softened
2 tablespoons grated Parmesan cheese
½ teaspoon dried basil leaves
½ teaspoon parsley flakes

Mix all ingredients. Brush on fish occasionally during cooking.

Garlic Butter

2 tablespoons margarine or butter, softened
½ teaspoon paprika
½ teaspoon dried oregano leaves
1 clove garlic, crushed
Dash of freshly ground pepper

Mix all ingredients. Brush on fish occasionally during cooking.

RED SPOON TIPS

Grilling is one of the most enjoyable and easy ways to cook food. Foods can simply be grilled to juicy perfection, or marinated for extra flavor and tenderness. They can be cooked in a flash, or slowly smoked to mouthwatering excitement.

There are several general items to be aware of when grilling. First, when grilling several different foods, make sure the height of the grill above the coals is appropriate for all of them. Second, salt food when it is done, not before (salt draws out the juices), and don't salt it over the grill (salt will corrode the metal). And finally, have a little patience when grilling. If you wait for coals to heat, you'll be off to a good start. Here is a brief introduction to a variety of popular grillworks.

The Grills

When shopping for a grill, consider how frequently it will be used and how sophisticated it needs to be. A very sturdy grill that seems expensive might be a sensible purchase if it is going to be in constant use for a number of years.

Grillworks are manufactured with numerous features. It is important to identify those features that would be particularly useful. Read on for a brief description of grillworks available today.

Braziers: These grills are simple and often nothing more than a shallow firebox to hold charcoal and a metal grill to hold the food. Braziers may have three or four long or short legs that are stationary or foldable (remember that *tripods* don't tip). Many models feature a sort of "Lazy Susan" cooking grill and/or grill supports at different heights. These help control the heat.

Brazier.

Covered Kettle Cookers: These charcoal-fired grills of heavy cast metal are made in a variety of sizes. The covered kettle is constructed along the lines of the brazier, with some sophisticated additions that include air vents or dampers (to control the heat) and such options as rib racks, holders for roasts, skewers with racks and motorized rotisseries.

Covered
Kettle
Cooker.

Gas Grills/Electric Grills: These grills are for people who are not interested in tending charcoal fires. Gas- or electric-fueled flame heats semipermanent briquets. These briquets act like coals, cooking the food by radiant heat. Food needn't be grilled over charcoal to have that "outdoors" flavor, since it is primarily the smoke created when drippings burn that accounts for most of the flavor.

Gas grills are either portable (fed by small propane tanks) or stationary (connected to a below-ground gas tank). Some models come with tank gauges that indicate fuel levels. Porcelain-coated gas grills are also available: They are corrosion-resistant and easy to clean. Electric grills must be connected to grounded electrical outlets or extensions, and therefore do not have the mobility of other grills.

Hibachis: These charcoal grills of Japanese design are made of heavy metal and sit only inches from the ground. Their small size makes them portable, which allows for on-the-spot cooking. The single hibachi is made to grill small amounts of food. However, double- and triple-grill models are available. Usually, these grills have convenient wood-covered handles.

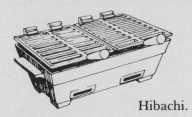

Hibachi.

Additional Cooking Equipment

Rotisseries: These are pieces of equipment or optional features that work with covered kettles, gas or electric grills or smokers. A rotisserie consists of a spit rod with supports. The spit rod looks something like an elongated fork with tines at either end.

Gas Grill.

Smokers: These are "slow-cookers," using charcoal or electricity. Wet hardwood chips burn on a bed of hot coals, producing smoke. A pan of water is then placed over the heat, which adds water vapor and creates a moist cooking environment.

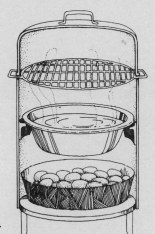

Smoker.

Starting the Grill

Grilling fires can be started in a variety of ways. One of the simplest is with liquid starter, following the manufacturer's directions. Liquid starter is poured over charcoal and allowed to soak in a few minutes before it is lit. (Never add liquid starter after lighting the charcoal.) Liquid starter is flammable and therefore it burns on the briquets themselves, giving them a chance to ignite. "Self-starting" charcoal briquets are made with a flammable compound, which makes them easy to light.

The manufacturers of gas and electric grills and smokers provide instructions that should be followed to the letter.

Tips for Charcoal Grilling

To begin, make certain that the briquets are dry. Damp charcoal may never catch fire. A little charcoal goes a long way. For 4 to 6 servings of a quick-cooking food (such as hamburger), use 20 to 30 briquets; 40 to 50 are sufficient for roasts, whole fish, pork and other longer-cooking foods. Anything that requires more than one hour of grilling time will need about 10 additional briquets per hour.

Arrange the briquets in a low pyramid (allowing for air to circulate). If using an electric starter, pyramid the briquets over the coil before plugging it in. Once the briquets have been started (about 8 to 12 minutes), unplug the starter. Then set it on a fireproof surface, out of the way. The coals will be ready for grilling in another 15 to 20 minutes.

If using liquid starter, follow the manufacturer's directions. After the starter has soaked the briquets for a few minutes, ignite the outer edges of the briquets. The coals are ready for grilling when they have a light, even coating of gray ash. If it is dark outside, they will glow a dusky red. Bright orange-red coals are too hot, black coals too cool, and a mixture of red and black coals often gives off an uneven amount of heat.

When the coals are ready, spread them out evenly into an area only slightly larger than the area to be covered by food on the grill. Check the temperature of the grill by placing your hand, palm down, near—but not touching—the grill. If the heat is so strong that you have to pull your hand away in 2 seconds or less, the coals are too hot. Wait another 5 to 10 minutes until your hand can take the heat for 4 to 5 seconds. This indicates the coals are at a medium heat level.

Keep the heat even throughout the cooking period. The heat can be raised by raking coals more closely together, knocking off some of the gray ash, opening the vents (if any) or even lowering the height of the cooking grill. To lower the heat, spread the coals out, partially close vents and raise the grill. Remember that cooking time will be shorter on hot, calm days than cool, windy ones.

Tips for Gas or Electric Grilling

Gas and electric grills start instantly, heat quickly, are easy to control and supply the desired cooking temperature, as long as it is needed. Heat the grill as per the manufacturer's instructions. In cool or windy weather, a higher temperature setting will speed up the cooking.

Heat is regulated by automatic controls. It can be adjusted further by covering or uncovering the grill, or adjusting the height of the cooking grill. Most gas grills have "fast-cooking" and "slow-cooking" spots; once the cook knows where they lie, they can be an advantage.

To make lava briquets last longer, turn them over occasionally, between cooking times, so that grease burns off them evenly.

Tips for Cooking on a Rotisserie

Cooking time is determined by the thickness of the food and the distance from the heat. For even cooking, make sure the food is balanced on the spit rod.

Tips for Cooking in a Smoker

Food in a smoker cooks very slowly and therefore uses far more charcoal than simple grilling over hot coals. Start a charcoal smoker as you would any charcoal grill, following the manufacturer's directions. Check periodically to make sure that the wood chips don't need to be replenished and that the water pan isn't dry. When smoke can no longer be seen coming from the vents, it is time to add a few more chips. Heat in a smoker is controlled by adjusting the vents and the height of the cooking rack. Different kinds of wood create different "flavors" of smoke. Hickory, fruitwood and green hardwood chips are popular "flavors." Oak, mesquite, pecan, grapevine cuttings and alder can also be used. Remember that wood must be thoroughly soaked in order to produce smoke.

Grilling Safety

To grill safely, follow these simple tips:

- Place the grill on level ground where it will stand steady.

- Never use gasoline or kerosene in place of liquid starter made especially for charcoal grilling.
- Never add liquid starter to briquets that have already been lit. The danger of the fire flaring up is great.
- Gas tanks must be handled with care. It is important to secure the tank when moving the grill. When the tank is connected to the regulator, do not let it tip.
- When attaching a gas tank to the grill, check the connection with liquid detergent. The appearance of bubbles indicates a leak.
- Store gas tanks and liquid starters away from the house.
- Grill only in well-ventilated areas, never in an enclosed space.
- Woods that are not suitable for smoking include pine, cedar, spruce and eucalyptus. Their smoke is acrid.
- Do not leave a fire unattended. Children should have supervision around grills.

How to Tell When Food Is Done

Most people have their own ideas about when meat is done. However, there are some safety standards to keep in mind. Except in the case of very experienced cooks, it is often not enough to judge doneness by the look or feel of the food. Follow recipe guidelines for cooking times and for internal temperatures, where applicable.

When using a meat thermometer, insert it so that the tip rests in the center of the thickest part of the meat, but does not touch bone or rest in fat. In the case of turkey, place the tip in the thickest part of the thigh. For additional indications of doneness after the minimum cooking time, press the meat lightly with protected fingers. If the juices run red, the food is not sufficiently cooked. If they run pink in the case of beef or lamb, that is fine for those who enjoy their meat rare. However, for pork or poultry, a few minutes more cooking time is necessary if the juices run pink.

Chicken is done when the juices run clear, the leg meat feels very soft between protected fingers and the leg of a whole bird moves easily. (These signs also apply to turkey, goose, duck, capon, Cornish game hens and quail.) Fish is done when the meat flakes easily with a fork. To test, insert a fork at an angle into the thickest part of the fish and twist gently.

Table of Internal Temperatures

Beef and Lamb	
rare	140°F
medium	160°F
well	170°F
Fish, fresh (not frozen)	175°F
Pork	
fresh cuts	170°F
smoked cuts:	
arm picnic (cook before eating)	170°F
loin or ham (cook before eating)	160°F
fully cooked ham, Canadian-style bacon or arm picnic	140°F
Turkey	185°F

Beef: All-time Favorite cuts for Grilling

STEAKS, ON THE GRILL (cook 4 to 5 inches from medium coals, turning once)

¾ inch thick	10 to 20 minutes
1 inch thick	18 to 25 minutes
1½ inches thick	25 to 35 minutes

ROASTS, ON THE ROTISSERIE (cook 4 inches from low heat)

Rare (140°F)	20 to 25 minutes per pound
Medium (160°F)	30 to 35 minutes per pound
Well (170°F)	40 minutes per pound

Entertaining Alfresco

Entertaining *alfresco*—in the open air—always brings forth a feeling of adventure. It hardly matters if the party takes place in an acre of wildflowers or two yards from the back door. Food always tastes terrific outside! There are just a few things to keep in mind when entertaining guests outdoors.

Have an alternate plan in the event that the weather doesn't cooperate. If it's clear in advance that the party can't be held outside, make sure that guests know where they are supposed to meet. Though it's a shame the plans have to change, at least there will be plenty of time to set up the party indoors. In the case of an unexpected downpour, have a nearby shelter in mind.

Insects can be dreadful pests. They are especially prevalent when the weather has been damp and hot for several days. Keep insect repellent handy. There are insect-repelling candles available, too, that discourage bugs with their waft of light smoke.

When entertaining farther than a brisk walk from the kitchen, it pays to make up a list of equipment needed:

- Plates
- Glasses
- Cutlery
- Serving utensils
- Small sharp kitchen or paring knife
- Napkins
- Bottle and can openers
- Matches
- Tablecloths/ground cloths
- Lights as needed: lanterns, votive candles, flashlights, torches, hurricane lamps
- Paper toweling (tuck some dampened paper toweling into a plastic bag)
- Insulated carriers/coolers (keep hot foods hot, cold foods cold)
- Large paper or plastic bags for collecting waste
- Insect repellent, as the season dictates
- And, of course, the grilling paraphernalia (pages 5–6)

Menus for the Grill

FINALLY FRIDAY

- Fiesta Burgers (page 12)
- Corn on the cob
- French fried onion rings
- Tin roof sundaes (vanilla ice cream with Spanish peanuts and chocolate sauce)

A TASTE OF TEXAS

- Texas Pork Steaks (page 34)
- Baked beans or buttery mashed potatoes
- Tossed green salad with green goddess dressing
- Barbecue Bread with Garlic-Chive Spread (page 85)
- Broiled Red River grapefruit

SEAFOOD BUFFET

- Red Snapper Fillets with Mustard Butter (page 69)
- Grilled Butterflied Shrimp (page 76)
- Mushrooms Lyonnaise (page 80)
- New potatoes in parsley butter
- Fresh sliced peaches with blueberries
- Crisp cookies

INDIAN SUMMER

- Curried Beef and Vegetable Kabobs (page 15)
- Grilled Eggplant (page 83)
- Pilaf with toasted almonds
- Sliced oranges and bananas

SUMMER KICK-OFF

- Smokehouse Spareribs (page 35)
- Grilled German Potato Salad (page 82)
- Ripe tomatoes with red onions
- Grilled Shortcake with fresh berries (page 87)

LIGHTLY DOES IT

- Wine-marinated Chicken (page 50)
- Grilled Corn (page 81)
- Chilled rice and garden vegetable salad
- Sesame Bread (page 84)
- Fresh fruit sorbet

Sensational Make-ahead Sides

Ratatouille Salad

1 small eggplant (about 1 pound), cut into ½-inch cubes
2 medium tomatoes, chopped (about 1½ cups)
1 medium zucchini, thinly sliced
1 small onion, sliced and separated into rings
1 small green pepper, chopped
⅓ cup snipped parsley
Basil Dressing (below)

Heat small amount salted water (½ teaspoon salt to 1 cup water) to boiling. Add eggplant. Cover and heat to boiling; reduce heat. Boil until tender, 5 to 8 minutes; drain. Cool.

Mix eggplant, tomatoes, zucchini, onion, green pepper and parsley; toss with Basil Dressing. Cover and refrigerate at least 4 hours. Serve on lettuce leaves, if desired.

BASIL DRESSING

ABOUT ⅓ CUP

⅓ cup olive or vegetable oil
2 tablespoons lemon juice
1 teaspoon salt
½ teaspoon dried basil leaves
½ teaspoon dry mustard
⅛ teaspoon pepper

Shake all ingredients in tightly covered jar.

Potato Salad

1 1/2 cups mayonnaise or salad dressing
1 tablespoon vinegar
1 tablespoon prepared mustard
1 teaspoon salt
1/4 teaspoon pepper
6 cups cubed, cooked potatoes (about 6
  medium potatoes), cooled slightly
2 medium stalks celery, chopped (about 1
  cup)
1 medium onion, chopped (about 1/2 cup)
4 hard-cooked eggs, chopped

Mix mayonnaise, vinegar, mustard, salt and pepper in 4-quart glass or plastic bowl. Add potatoes, celery and onion; toss. Stir in eggs. Cover and refrigerate at least 4 hours.

CALIFORNIA-STYLE POTATO SALAD: Omit eggs. Stir in 1 can (4 ounces) chopped green chilies, drained, with the vegetables. Just before serving, stir in 2 avocados, chopped, and 2 tomatoes, chopped.

GARDEN POTATO SALAD: Stir in 1/2 cup thinly sliced radishes, 1/2 cup chopped cucumber and 1/2 cup chopped green pepper. Garnish with tomato wedges.

Egg and Rice Casserole

8 SERVINGS

3 cups hot cooked rice
2 cups shredded Colby cheese (about 8
  ounces)
1 package (10 ounces) frozen green peas,
  thawed
1 jar (2 ounces) diced pimiento, drained
1/4 cup sliced green onions (with tops)
1 1/2 teaspoons salt
1/2 teaspoon dried dill weed
4 eggs, beaten
1 1/2 cups milk

Mix rice, cheese, peas, pimiento, onions, salt and dill weed. Spread in greased 12 × 7 1/2 × 2-inch baking dish. Mix eggs and milk; pour over rice mixture. Cook uncovered in 350° oven until set, about 45 minutes.

NOTE: Before cooking, cover and refrigerate no longer than 24 hours. To serve, cook uncovered in 350° oven about 1 hour.

Sweet-and-Sour Beet Salad

8 SERVINGS

½ cup vinegar
⅓ cup sugar
½ teaspoon grated orange peel
¼ cup orange juice
¼ teaspoon salt
2 cans (16 ounces each) sliced beets, drained
Salad greens
Snipped parsley (optional)

Heat vinegar, sugar, orange peel, orange juice and salt to boiling in 2-quart saucepan, stirring occasionally; reduce heat. Simmer uncovered 5 minutes. Stir in beets. Cover and refrigerate at least 8 hours. Serve on salad greens; sprinkle with snipped parsley.

Shady Glade Salad

8 SERVINGS

No-Oil Dressing (below)
3 medium oranges, pared, sliced and cut into halves
5 medium radishes, sliced
2 stalks celery, cut diagonally into slices
3 green onions, sliced
1 medium green pepper, cut into 1-inch strips
1 medium cucumber, sliced

Prepare No-Oil Dressing; pour on remaining ingredients in shallow glass or plastic dish. Cover and refrigerate at least 1 hour. Drain salad before serving.

NO-OIL DRESSING

ABOUT 1⅓ CUPS

⅔ cup water
½ cup sugar
⅓ cup vinegar
½ teaspoon salt
¼ teaspoon pepper

Shake all ingredients in tightly covered jar.

Four-Bean Salad

6 SERVINGS

Spicy Herb Dressing (below)
1 can (16 ounces) cut green beans,
  drained
1 can (16 ounces) wax beans, drained
1 can (15 ounces) kidney beans, drained
1 can (15½ ounces) garbanzo beans,
  drained
½ cup finely chopped green pepper
½ cup sliced pitted ripe olives
¼ cup sliced green onions
¼ cup snipped parsley
1 jar (2 ounces) sliced pimiento, drained
  and finely chopped
Lettuce

Prepare Spicy Herb Dressing. Place remaining ingredients except lettuce in large bowl; toss with dressing. Cover and refrigerate at least 4 hours. Drain salad, reserving dressing. Serve in lettuce-lined bowl. (Dressing can be refrigerated and used again within 1 week.)

SPICY HERB DRESSING

ABOUT 1½ CUPS

½ cup sugar
½ cup wine vinegar
½ cup vegetable oil
1½ teaspoons salt
½ teaspoon dry mustard
½ teaspoon pepper
½ teaspoon red pepper sauce
¼ teaspoon dried basil leaves
¼ teaspoon garlic powder

Shake all ingredients in tightly covered jar.

Creamy Coleslaw

Creamy Dressing (below)
6 cups finely shredded green cabbage
  (about 1 1/2 pounds)
1/3 cup chopped onion
1/3 cup chopped cucumber

Prepare Creamy Dressing; toss with remaining ingredients.

CREAMY DRESSING

ABOUT 1 CUP

2/3 cup mayonnaise or salad dressing
2 tablespoons sugar
2 tablespoons vinegar
1 tablespoon milk
1/2 teaspoon salt
1/8 teaspoon paprika

Mix all ingredients; refrigerate at least 1 hour.

Bulgur and Tomato Salad

6 TO 8 SERVINGS

2 cups boiling water
1 cup bulgur wheat
2 cups cherry tomatoes, cut into halves
3 tablespoons lemon juice
2 tablespoons snipped fresh mint leaves
  or 1 teaspoon dried mint leaves
2 tablespoons snipped chives
2 tablespoons snipped parsley
1 teaspoon salt
1/4 teaspoon lemon pepper
Cherry tomatoes
Parsley

Pour water on bulgur; let stand 15 minutes. Drain. Mix bulgur, 2 cups tomatoes, the lemon juice, mint leaves, chives, 2 tablespoons parsley, the salt and lemon pepper. Cover and refrigerate 2 hours. Garnish with tomatoes and parsley.

INDEX

Acorn Squash, Stuffed, 83
Almond Glaze, 90
Apples
  Alfresco, 87
  on Skewers, Veal and, 48

Barbecue Bread, 85
Barbecued Ribs, 36
Bean Salad, Four, 107
Beef, 9–28
  cuts and cooking times, 102
  Hamburgers. *See* Hamburgers
  Kabobs, Curried Beef and Vegetable, 15
  Liver Venetian, 23
  London Broil, Barbecued, 22
  Roast, Pepper and Onion, 28
  Roast, Rotisserie, 27
  Rump Roast, Marinated, 26
  on Skewers, 18
  Short Ribs, Tomato-glazed, 23
  Steak au Poivre, 19
  Steak, Beer-barbecued, 18
  Steak, Charcoal-broiled, 19
  Steak, Ranch, 22
  Tenderloin Roast, 26
Beer-barbecued Steak, 18
Beet Salad, Sweet-and-Sour, 106
Blue Cheese Spread, 85
Braziers, 97
Bread, 84–86, 90
  Barbecue, 85
  Cheese Loaf, Stringy, 90
  Parmesan Slices, 84
  Sesame, 84
  spreads for, 85–86
Bulgur and Tomato Salad, 108
Butters, flavored, 60, 69, 85–86

Cake
  Grilled Shortcake, 87
  Zucchini-Nut, 90
Caper Sauce, 70
Carrot and Onion Kabobs, 81
Casserole, Egg and Rice, 105
Charcoal briquets, 97, 98, 99
Charcoal-broiled Steak, 19
Cheese Loaf, Stringy 90
Cheeseburgers, 13, 15
Chicken
  Afghanistan, 51
  Caribbean Chicken Legs, 54
  Fiery, 50
  Garlic, on the Rotisserie, 57
  Grilled, Simple, 49
  Honey-glazed, 50
  Italian Style, 57
  Lemon, 49
  Oriental Chicken Wings, 51
  Paprika Chicken Breasts, 55
  Teriyaki Chicken Breasts, 55
  Wine-marinated, 50

Cinnamon Whipped Cream, 87
Cod, Dilled, 68
Coleslaw, Creamy, 108
Confetti Fish in Foil, 68
Coriander Sauce, 61
Corn, Grilled, 81
  Roasted, 60
Corn in the Husk, 81
Cornish Hens, 101
  Rotisserie, 56
  Wine-basted, 56
Crab-stuffed Rainbow Trout, 75

Desserts, 87–90
Dilled Cod, 68
Doneness of food, 101
Duck, 100
  Savory, 61

Egg and Rice Casserole, 105
Eggplant, Grilled, 83
Entertaining Alfresco, 102

Fiery Chicken, 50
Fish, 64–79
  Breaded, Grilled, 70–71
  Cod, Dilled, 68
  Confetti, in Foil, 68
  Fillets, Bacon-wrapped, 65
  Fillets, Lime, 65
  Fillets, Teriyaki, 65
  in Foil, Confetti, 68
  Rice-stuffed, 75
  Salmon, Smoked, 71
  Snapper Fillets, Red, with Flavored Butters, 69
  Snapper, Mediterranean, 69
  Sole in Foil, 64
  Steaks with Chives and Lemon, 71
  Steaks, Monterey, 70
  Sticks, Breaded Grilled, 70–71
  Trout, Crab-stuffed Rainbow, 75
  Vegetables, and, 74
Four-Bean Salad, 107
Frankfurters,
  Glazed, 29
  Stuffed, 29

Garden Vegetable Stuffing, 74
Garlic
  Butter Spread, 86
  Chicken on the Rotisserie, 57
  Chive Spread, 85
  Shrimp, 76
German Potato Salad, Grilled, 82
Glazed Franks, 29
Grilled Breaded Fish Fillets, 70–71
Grilled Butterflied Shrimp, 76
Grilled Corn, 81
Grilled Eggplant, 83
Grilled Lamb Chops, 45

Grilled Lobster Tails, 77
Grilled Pineapple, 54
Grilled Pork Chops, 30
Grilled Shortcake, 87
Grilled Tomatoes, 61
Grilling, tips and tools, 5–6, 97–103
Grills
 cleaning, 6–7
 types of, 6, 97–99

Ham
 on the Rotisserie, Peachy, 41
 Smoked, with Maple Glaze, 35
Hamburgers, 9–15
 Cheese, Deluxe 13
 Colossal, 15
 Fiesta, 12
 Filled, 13
 Lemon, 14
 Supreme, 9
 Tortilla, 14
Herb–Cheese Butter Spread, 86
Herb–Lemon Butter Spread, 86
Hibachis, 98
Honey-glazed Chicken, 50
Hot dogs. See Frankfurters

Italian Sausage Kabobs, 34
Italian Style, Chicken, 57
Italian-style Zucchini, 83

Kabobs, 80
 Curried Beef and Vegetable, 15
 Lamb and Vegetable, 44
 Onion and Carrot, 81
 Sausage, Italian, 34
 Scallop, 77
 Vegetable, 80
 Vegetable, Smoky, 80

Lamb, 44–45
 Chops, Grilled, 45
 Kabobs, Lamb and Vegetable, 44
 Leg of, Barbecue, 44
Lemon Burgers, 14
Lemon Butter, 69
Lemon Chicken, 49
Lemon Potatoes, 82
Lime Fish Fillets, 65
Liver Venetian, 23
Lobster Tails, Grilled, 77
London Broil, Barbecued, 22

Marinated Pork Chops, 30
Marinated Rump Roast, 26
Mediterranean Snapper, 69
Menus, 103
Monterey Fish Steaks, 70
Mushroom(s)
 Lyonnaise, 80
 topping, 13
Mustard Butter, 69

Onion and Carrot Kabobs, 81
Onion Butter Spread, 86
Oriental Chicken Wings, 51

Paprika, Chicken Breasts, 55
Parmesan
 Cheese Spread, 85
 Slices, 84
Peachy Ham on the Rotisserie, 41
Peanut Butter Spread, Creamy, 85
Peanut-stuffed Pork Chops, 31
Pepper and Onion Roast, 28
Pineapple, Grilled, 54
Pork, 29–41
 Ribs, Barbecued, 36
 Ribs, Spit-barbecued, 37
 Chops, Grilled, 30
 Chops, Marinated, 30
 Chops, Peanut-stuffed, 31
 Chops, Smoked, 31
 Ham. See Ham
 Roast, and Orange Sauce, 40
 Roast, Polynesian Rotisserie, 41
 Spareribs, Smoked Chutney, 37
 Spareribs, Smokehouse, 35
 Steaks, Texas, 34
Potato(es)
 Lemon, 82
 Roasted, 60
 Salad, 105
 Salad, Grilled German, 82
Poultry, 49–63. See also specific types.

Ratatouille Salad, 104
Red Snapper Fillets with Flavored Butters, 69
Red Spoon Tips, 97–108
Ribs
 Beef, Short, Tomato-glazed, 23
 Pork, Barbecued, 36
 Pork, Spit-barbecued, 37
 Spareribs, Smoked Chutney, 37
 Spareribs, Smokehouse, 35
Rice Casserole, Egg and, 105
Rice-stuffed Fish, 75
Roast. See specific types.
Roasted Corn, 60
Roasted Potatoes, 60
Roast Pork and Orange Sauce, 40
Rotisserie(s), 97, 98
 Beef Roast, 27
 Cornish Hens, 56
 Garlic Chicken on the, 57
 Ham, Peachy, 41
 Pork, Polynesian, 41
Rump Roast, Marinated, 26

Salad dressings
 Basil, 104
 Creamy, 108
 No-Oil, 106
 Spicy Herb, 107
Salads, 104–108
 Bulgur and Tomato, 108
 Coleslaw, Creamy, 108
 Four-Bean, 107
 Garden Potato, 105
 Potato, 105
 Potato, Grilled German, 82
 Potato, California-style, 105
 Ratatouille, 104

Salads *(cont.)*
  Shady Glade, 106
  Sweet-and-Sour Beet, 106
Salmon, Smoked, 71
Salting of food, 97
Sauce(s)
  Avocado, 70
  Caper, 70
  Cocktail, 95
  Cucumber, 95
  Garlic Butter, 96
  Horseradish, Zippy, 95
  Lemon Butter, 69
  Mustard Butter, 69
  Parmesan Butter, 96
  Thyme Butter, 60
  Barbecue Sauce(s), 94
  Chef's Special, 92
  Coriander, 61
  Easy, 94
  Herb Wine, 93
  Honey-Herb, 93
  Honey-Mustard, 92
  Lemon, 91
  Mint-Garlic, 45
  Orange, 93
  Orange-Ginger, 45
  Parisian, 91
  Red Currant, 45
  Smoky, 94
  Sweet-and-Sour, 36
  Texas, 92
  Tomato, Peppy, 27
  Wine, 27
Sausage Kabobs, Italian, 34
Savory Duckling, 61
Scallop Kabobs, 77
Sesame Bread, 84
Shady Glade Salad, 106
Shellfish, 76–77
Short Ribs, Tomato-glazed, 23
Shortcake, Grilled, 87
Shrimp
  Garlic, 76
  Grilled Butterflied, 76
Simple Grilled Chicken, 49
Smoked Chutney Spareribs, 37
Smoked Ham with Maple Glaze, 35
Smoked Pork Chops, 31
Smoked Salmon, 71
Smokehouse Spareribs, 35
Smokers, 98, 99
Smoky Vegetable Kabobs, 80
Sole in Foil, 64

Spareribs. *See* Ribs
  Smoked Chutney, 37
  Smokehouse, 35
Spit-barbecued Ribs, 37
Spreads for bread, 85–86
Squash
  Acorn, Stuffed, 83
  Zucchini, Italian style, 83
Steak
  Beer-barbecued, 18
  Charcoal-broiled, 19
  au Poivre, 19
  Pork, Texas, 34
  Ranch, 22
Stuffing for Fish, Garden Vegetable, 74
Stringy Cheese Loaf, 90
Stuffed Acorn Squash, 83
Sweet-and-Sour
  Beet Salad, 106
  Sauce, 36

Tarragon Butter Spread, 86
Temperatures, table of internal, 101
Tenderloin Roast, Beef, 26
Teriyaki
  Chicken Breasts, 55
  Fillets, 65
Texas Pork Steaks, 34
Thermometers, 6, 101
Thyme Butter, 60
Tomato-glazed Short Ribs, 23
Tomatoes, Grilled, 61
Toppings
  Avocado, 12
  Mushroom, 13
Trout, Crab-stuffed Rainbow, 75
Turkey and Vegetable Barbecue, 60

Utensils for grilling, 5–6

Veal and Apples on Skewers, 48
Vegetable(s), 80–96
  and Curried Beef Kabobs, 15
  fish stuffed with, 71
  grilled or roasted, 60–61
  Kabobs, 80
  Kabobs with Lamb, 44

Wine-basted Hens, 56
Wine-marinated Chicken, 50

Zucchini
  Italian-style, 83
  Nut Cake, 90

Credits

V.P., Associate Publisher: Anne M. Zeman
Project Editor: Rebecca W. Atwater
Creative Director: J.C. Suarès
Photographer: Anthony Johnson
Designer: Patricia Fabricant
Production Editor: Kimberly Ebert

112